# The
# Divine Outline
## of
# History

# THE DIVINE OUTLINE
# OF HISTORY

## DISPENSATIONS AND THE CHURCH

### R. B. THIEME, JR.

R. B. THIEME, JR., BIBLE MINISTRIES
HOUSTON, TEXAS

## FINANCIAL POLICY

There is no charge for any material from R. B. Thieme, Jr., Bible Ministries. Anyone who desires Bible teaching can receive our books, MP3 CDs, and tapes without obligation. God provides Bible doctrine. We wish to reflect His grace.

R. B. Thieme, Jr., Bible Ministries is a grace ministry and operates entirely on voluntary contributions. There is no price list for books or tapes. No money is requested. When gratitude for the Word of God motivates a believer to give, he has the privilege of contributing to the dissemination of Bible doctrine.

This book is edited from the lectures and unpublished notes of R. B. Thieme, Jr.

A catalogue of available audio recordings and publications will be provided upon request.

R. B. Thieme, Jr., Bible Ministries
P. O. Box 460829, Houston, Texas 77056-8829
www.rbthieme.org

Printed in the United States of America

ISBN 1-55764-043-2

# Contents

Preface . . . . . . . . . . . . . . . . . . . . . . . . . . . . . . . . . . . . . . . . . . . . . . *ix*

*Chapter One: The Believer's Place in Time*

The Great Question . . . . . . . . . . . . . . . . . . . . . . . . . . . . . . . . . . . . . 1
Dispensations Defined . . . . . . . . . . . . . . . . . . . . . . . . . . . . . . . . . . 3
Six Dispensations . . . . . . . . . . . . . . . . . . . . . . . . . . . . . . . . . . . . . . 4
The Reason for Dispensations . . . . . . . . . . . . . . . . . . . . . . . . . . . . 6
Times and Epochs . . . . . . . . . . . . . . . . . . . . . . . . . . . . . . . . . . . . . . 7
Ages and Administrations . . . . . . . . . . . . . . . . . . . . . . . . . . . . . . . . 10
Dispensations as Taught by Paul . . . . . . . . . . . . . . . . . . . . . . . . . . 12

*Chapter Two: An Outline of Dispensations*

Establishing a Framework . . . . . . . . . . . . . . . . . . . . . . . . . . . . . . . . 16
Respect for Divine Distinctions . . . . . . . . . . . . . . . . . . . . . . . . . . . 19

*Chapter Three: The Theocentric Dispensations*

The Age of the Gentiles . . . . . . . . . . . . . . . . . . . . . . . . . . . . . . . . . 22
    Positive Volition . . . . . . . . . . . . . . . . . . . . . . . . . . . . . . . . . . . . 22
    Negative Volition . . . . . . . . . . . . . . . . . . . . . . . . . . . . . . . . . . . . 24
    Jewish Patriarchs . . . . . . . . . . . . . . . . . . . . . . . . . . . . . . . . . . . . 26
The Dispensation of Israel . . . . . . . . . . . . . . . . . . . . . . . . . . . . . . . 28
    God's Chosen Nation . . . . . . . . . . . . . . . . . . . . . . . . . . . . . . . . . 28

Divine Covenants with Israel . . . . . . . . . . . . . . . . . . . . . . . . . . . 31
Conditional and Unconditional Covenants . . . . . . . . . . . . . . . . 32
The Client Nation . . . . . . . . . . . . . . . . . . . . . . . . . . . . . . . . . . . . 34

*Chapter Four: The Christocentric Dispensations*

The Dispensation of the Hypostatic Union . . . . . . . . . . . . . . . . . 37
Hypostatic Union Defined . . . . . . . . . . . . . . . . . . . . . . . . . . . . . 37
Interpreting the Teachings of Christ . . . . . . . . . . . . . . . . . . . . . 39
Freedom of Choice under God's Plan . . . . . . . . . . . . . . . . . . . . 41
Accuracy in Interpretation . . . . . . . . . . . . . . . . . . . . . . . . . . . . . 43
Different Messages for Different Audiences . . . . . . . . . . . . . 43
Teaching for Present and Future Hearers . . . . . . . . . . . . . . 45
The Incarnation as a Separate Dispensation . . . . . . . . . . . . . . 48
Four Reasons . . . . . . . . . . . . . . . . . . . . . . . . . . . . . . . . . . . . . 48
God Revealed in Christ . . . . . . . . . . . . . . . . . . . . . . . . . . . . . 49
The Great Power Experiment . . . . . . . . . . . . . . . . . . . . . . . . 50
Giving Definition to Other Dispensations . . . . . . . . . . . . . . 52
Christ the Cornerstone . . . . . . . . . . . . . . . . . . . . . . . . . . . . . 53
The Separation of Israel and the Church . . . . . . . . . . . . . . . . 56
Fulfillment of the Mosaic Law . . . . . . . . . . . . . . . . . . . . . . . 56
The Law of Christ . . . . . . . . . . . . . . . . . . . . . . . . . . . . . . . . . 58
Transition between Divine Administrations . . . . . . . . . . . . . 59
Common Principles in Different Codes . . . . . . . . . . . . . . . . . 60
The Continuing Value of the Mosaic Law . . . . . . . . . . . . . . 61
The Dispensation of the Church . . . . . . . . . . . . . . . . . . . . . . . . . 63
The Church in Biblical Perspective . . . . . . . . . . . . . . . . . . . . . 63
The Epoch of the Royal Family of God . . . . . . . . . . . . . . . . . . 64
Gentile Client Nations . . . . . . . . . . . . . . . . . . . . . . . . . . . . . . . 66
Precanon and Postcanon Eras . . . . . . . . . . . . . . . . . . . . . . . . . 68

*Chapter Five: The Eschatological Dispensations*

The Tribulation . . . . . . . . . . . . . . . . . . . . . . . . . . . . . . . . . . . . . . . 71
The Millennium . . . . . . . . . . . . . . . . . . . . . . . . . . . . . . . . . . . . . . . 74
The Reign of Christ . . . . . . . . . . . . . . . . . . . . . . . . . . . . . . . . . . 74
The Conclusion of the Millennium . . . . . . . . . . . . . . . . . . . . . . 77

*Chapter Six: The Uniqueness of the Church Age*

Continuity and Change ................................... 79
The *Politeuma* Metaphor ............................... 82
The Baptism of the Holy Spirit ......................... 85
  A New Spiritual Species in Christ ..................... 85
  Conformed to the Image of Christ ..................... 87
  Misconceptions of the Baptism of the Spirit ........... 91
  Sharing All Christ Has and Is ........................ 92
The Protocol Plan of God ............................... 93
Mystery Doctrine ...................................... 96
The Portfolio of Invisible Assets ...................... 97
  The Believer's Wealth Taught by Analogy ............... 97
  Escrow Blessings ..................................... 99
    Inheritance Reserved in Heaven ..................... 99
    Blessings for Time and Eternity .................... 101
    Undistributed Blessings and the Glory of God ........ 102
  Computer Assets ..................................... 104
    A Modern Analogy .................................. 104
    Divine Sovereignty and Christian Freedom ........... 106
  Enlarging the Portfolio with Secondary Assets ........ 109
  Volitional Assets ................................... 111
    Good Decisions from a Position of Strength ......... 111
    The Visible and the Invisible ..................... 112
    Changes in Positive Volition ...................... 114
    Volition Remains Free ............................. 115
    The Role of Encouragement ......................... 116
  Production Assets ................................... 117
  Assets for Undeserved Suffering ..................... 119
  Personnel Assets in the Church Age Portfolio ........ 121
The Equality Factor ................................... 122
Royal Commissions ..................................... 124
The Indwelling of the Trinity ......................... 126
  God Residing in the Believer ........................ 126
  The Indwelling of the Father ........................ 127
  The Indwelling of Jesus Christ ...................... 128
  The Indwelling of the Holy Spirit ................... 131
The Availability of Divine Power ...................... 133

The Absence of Prophecy ............................... 134
Invisible Heroes ...................................... 137

*Chapter Seven: Epilogue*

After Salvation, What? ................................ 140

*Indices*

Scripture Index ...................................... 143
Subject Index ........................................ 155

# *Preface*

Before you begin your Bible study, if you are a believer in the Lord Jesus Christ, be sure you have named your sins privately to God the Father.

> If we confess our [known] sins, He is faithful and righteous to forgive us our [known] sins and to cleanse us from all [unknown, or forgotten sins] unrighteousness. (1 John 1:9)

You will then be in fellowship with God, filled with the Holy Spirit, and ready to learn Bible doctrine from the Word of God.

> "God is spirit, and those who worship Him must worship in [the filling of the] spirit and [biblical] truth." (John 4:24)

If you have never personally believed in the Lord Jesus Christ as your Savior, the issue is not naming your sins. The issue is faith alone in Christ alone.

> "He who believes in the Son has eternal life; but he who does not obey [the command to believe in] the Son shall not see life, but the wrath of God abides on him." (John 3:36)

THE WORD OF GOD is alive and powerful, sharper than any two-edged sword, piercing even to the dividing asunder of the soul and the spirit, and of the joints and the marrow, and is a critic of thoughts and intents of the heart. (Heb. 4:12)

All Scripture is God-breathed, and is profitable for doctrine, for reproof, for correction, for instruction in righteousness; that the man of God might be mature, thoroughly furnished unto all good works. (2 Tim. 3:16–17)

Study to show thyself approved unto God, a workman that needeth not to be ashamed, rightly dividing the word of truth. (2 Tim. 2:15)

*Chapter One*

# THE BELIEVER'S PLACE IN TIME

## THE GREAT QUESTION

WHAT IS THE CHRISTIAN'S PURPOSE on earth? Every believer in Jesus Christ should ask himself this question. After salvation, what?

Eternal salvation becomes an accomplished fact at the moment of faith in Christ. Heaven is absolutely guaranteed for anyone who has believed in Christ as Savior (Rom. 8:38–39; 1 Pet. 1:4–5). But the quality of the believer's life on earth depends on his execution of God's plan *after* salvation. Impact and blessings in time and eternity depend on fulfilling God's plan in time. The question becomes emphatic. What is God's plan for the believer following that initial instant of personal faith in Christ? God freely gives "all things" after providing salvation (Rom. 8:32). What are they? After salvation, what?

The simplified answer: Learn Bible doctrine! The Bible reveals God's Person and plan. Only through knowledge of God can anyone appreciate, love, and worship Him. As Christians we are commanded to "renovate [our] thinking" with divine viewpoint thinking so God's gracious purpose can be fulfilled in and through our lives (Rom. 12:2; Eph. 1:18; 4:22–24).

God's purpose for the postsalvation life of the believer calls for spiritual growth (2 Pet. 3:18). The Christian is kept alive on earth to fulfill his destiny, which is to become a mature believer, a spiritual winner, a "mature person to the measure of the maturity which belongs to the fulness of Christ" (Eph. 4:13–16). Each believer's life becomes a unique expression of the glory of God in both time and eternity (Rom. 8:29–30; 9:23–24), but only the *mature* believer glorifies God by receiving the highest and best that God has prepared for him (Rom. 6:1–2*a*; 1 John 1:5—2:6). Divine blessings that the Christian can understand and experience and the overt manifestations of the Christian way of life come as *results* of spiritual growth. The *means* of spiritual growth is the believer's consistent reception, retention, and recall of Bible doctrine through all the circumstances of his life.

Bible doctrine is teaching. It is the content of the Word of God, which God designed to be communicated to the believer so that it becomes the measure of his thinking (Rom. 12:3; 2 Tim. 3:16–17) and the source of his mental attitude (Phil. 2:5; Heb. 4:16). Doctrine is the body of orthodox teaching, which is drawn from Scripture and which serves as the standard for truth. Pastors have a spiritual gift for teaching Bible doctrine to their congregations (Eph. 4:8, 11–13). The pastor is responsible before God to diligently study the Bible in order to accurately handle the word of truth (2 Tim. 2:15). Doctrine is determined by:

1. *interpreting the text* in its historical context, in terms of its author's intent and its original audience, as well as in light of the times and places in which it was written;
2. *categorizing biblical subjects* by comparing all pertinent passages;
3. *exegeting the Scriptures* in their original languages.

The importance of Bible doctrine can hardly be overestimated. Why does God go so far as to magnify His Word above His Person (Ps. 138:2)? His Word reveals His nature and essence. Only the Scriptures allow us to glimpse God's absolute character and to love the revealed member of the Godhead, who is Jesus Christ (John 1:18). Bible doctrine is called the "mind of Christ" (1 Cor. 2:16). It is absolute truth, the very thinking of Jesus Christ (Phil. 2:5). "Though [we] have not seen Him, [we] love Him" when we learn who and what He is and begin to share His frame of reference (1 Pet. 1:8).

Understanding God's Word is the root of all Christian virtues. Transformation of the believer's life occurs on the inside, in the inner person, in the soul (Rom. 12:2). His persistent intake and application of Bible doctrine enlarge his capacities for life, for love, for service, for blessings, for happiness (2 Cor. 9:7–8). God's "greater grace" fills up the mature believer's greater capacities "to all the fulness of God" (Eph. 3:19; James 4:6; cf., Rom. 8:32). In so blessing the believer, God is glorified (Eph. 1:3).

Since Bible doctrine is so vitally important, the believer needs to understand an essential fact about the Word of God. Bible doctrine is *dispensational*. The concept of dispensations, therefore, is a key to understanding the whole realm of Bible doctrine.

## DISPENSATIONS DEFINED

A dispensation is a period of human history defined in terms of divine revelation. According to the Bible, history is a sequence of divine administrations. These consecutive eras reflect the unfolding of God's plan for mankind. They constitute the divine viewpoint of history and the theological interpretation of history. The doctrine of dispensations is the vehicle by which believers living at a specific time can orient to God's will, plan, and purpose for their lives.

God never changes. In the essence of God there is "no variation, or shifting shadow" (James 1:17). Change, however, is an integral characteristic of the administration of His plan for creation. But God is never impulsive or arbitrary. The changes He incorporates into His plan are designed to attain His unchangeable purpose (Heb. 6:17).

In different periods of human history, the biblical answer to "After salvation, what?" involves different mechanics and procedures. The doctrine of dispensations recognizes these differences as well as the continuities that run from one period to the next. This doctrine, therefore, becomes essential for understanding the believer's postsalvation experience. Knowledge of dispensations enables the individual believer to handle the word of truth accurately and to appreciate the magnificent grace of God both in its particular provisions and in its overall objectives. In contrast, failure to distinguish one biblical era from another creates apparent contradictions in divine mandates, prevents the believer from understanding current divine guidance, and thus retards his all-important spiritual growth.

Any study of the Bible must deal with the distinction between Israel and the Church. This contrast, which is a recurring theme in the New Testament (Acts 10:45; Rom. 11:25; Gal. 6:15; Eph. 2:11–22; Heb. 3:5–6), is the starting point in the doctrine of dispensations. What makes the separation of Israel and the Church so significant? The phenomenon that divides these two dispensations is the first advent of Christ. The Lord Jesus Christ makes all the difference. He is the key to the divine interpretation of history (Eph. 3:10–11; Rev. 1:8). The doctrine of dispensations spotlights Him, as we shall see.

Theologians may debate the issue of where precisely to divide the dispensations on the time line of human history. Some disagree on how to classify biblical distinctions, thus arriving at different numbers of dispensations. Ministers may stress certain aspects of the doctrine while neglecting others. Indeed, some theologians reject the entire doctrine of dispensations in order to perpetuate a tradition or justify a particular emphasis. But standing firm amid human controversies, the criterion for identifying the dispensations must always be what the Bible says, the very text of Scripture. The recognition of historical eras in the Bible unlocks the Scriptures, revealing profound truths with tremendous positive impact on our lives. When biblical distinctions are overlooked, particularly those between Israel and the Church, there are adverse practical and theological repercussions.[1]

## SIX DISPENSATIONS

Human history may be classified into six dispensations. These six can be grouped into three categories of two dispensations each. The theocentric, or pre-Incarnation, dispensations are the Age of the Gentiles and the Age of Israel, which occurred "long ago" before God had "spoken to us in His Son" (Heb. 1:1–2). The *christocentric* dispensations begin with the first advent of Christ, called the Dispensation of

---

1.  See pages 79–82.

| THEOCENTRIC | | CHRISTOCENTRIC | | ESCHATOLOGICAL | |
|---|---|---|---|---|---|
| Age of Gentiles | Age of Israel | Hypostatic Union | Church Age | Tribulation | Millennium |

**THE DISPENSATIONS OF HUMAN HISTORY**

the Hypostatic Union, and continue with the Church Age, which is the present dispensation. The Church carries out to completion the precedent established in our Lord's first advent. Finally, the *eschatological* dispensations (eschatology is the study of the final destiny of the human race) that the Bible prophesies and promises for the end of history are the Tribulation and Millennium.

God's unified, integrated, unchanging purpose for human history calls for many expressions of His grace. In every dispensation God has a particular plan for the believer's postsalvation way of life. He graciously provides the means for executing that plan, and the Bible reveals these various provisions. Salvation itself, however, is appropriated in only one way throughout human history—by grace through faith alone in Christ alone (Gen. 15:6; Acts 16:31; Rom. 3:22, 30; Eph. 2:8–9). In every dispensation there is only one Savior, our Lord Jesus Christ, as He is revealed in that dispensation (John 14:6). Faith in Christ secures an eternal relationship with God.

> "And there is salvation in no one else; for there is no other name under heaven that has been given among men, by which we must be saved." (Acts 4:12, NASB)[2]

The Savior's name has different forms in different languages. In Hebrew His name is *YHWH* (יהוה, *Yahweh*) a word considered too sacred to pronounce, so He is called אֲדֹנָי (*Adonai*). He appeared in many forms before His incarnation, including the burning bush, the cloud, the pillar of fire, and the Angel of *Yahweh*. He has many functional titles as well, like Messiah, Son of David, Lord of the Armies, or Prince of Peace. In the Greek of the New Testament, He is Χριστός (*Christos*) or κύριος (*kurios*) or Ἰησοῦς (*Iesous*) or any combination of the three. We know Him in Modern English as the Lord Jesus Christ. The Gospel of Christ is revealed to everyone who desires to

---

2. Unless indicated, Scripture quotations are my translations of the Hebrew and Greek texts. References marked NASB are quoted from the New American Standard Bible. Bracketed commentary correlates the quotation with its context or the discussion at hand.

know God.[3] God reveals Christ in many ways throughout the ages, but faith in Him is the only way of eternal salvation.

## THE REASON FOR DISPENSATIONS

Many principles, policies, and procedures that God establishes remain constant throughout history. But no careful student of the Bible can overlook certain changes that distinguish one epoch of biblical history from another. Why does God alter His administration of human history? He does so to reveal His unchanging glory, wisdom, and power under different conditions. From God's eternal perspective the ultimate in this long and varied demonstration of His character is the relationship between Christ and the Church, in which the believer is in union with Christ (Eph. 1:17–23; 3:10, 21). The explanation for this multifaceted divine revelation which unfolds throughout human history lies in an ancient conflict.

Before human history began, Satan revolted against God (Isa. 14:13–14). Satan and the host of angels who joined his revolution evidently were brought to trial and convicted (Ezek. 28:16–18), for their sentence is recorded in Scripture (Matt. 25:41). The sentence of fallen angels to "eternal fire" was pronounced *before* mankind existed. Why, then, was the execution of the sentence postponed until *after* human history ends (Rev. 20:10)?

Satan objected to God's verdict, just as he continues to contend against God. Any objection to perfect divine judgment slanders the character of God. In a momentous action, God convened an appeal trial in which He would demonstrate His perfect character (Ps. 145:21; Zech. 3:1–10; Luke 2:14; Rom. 9:23; 11:25–36) while allowing Satan every opportunity to prove his own case (Job 1:12; 2:6; Matt. 4:1–11). God created mankind to resolve the angelic conflict. In human history, for our benefit and for the benefit of the angels, God magnificently answers every aspect of Satan's objection in the prehistoric trial. Simultaneously, Satan is attempting to prove himself equal with God (Isa.

---

3. R. B. Thieme, Jr., *Heathenism* (Houston: R. B. Thieme, Jr., Bible Ministries, 2001, second impression). Hereafter, cross-references to my books will cite only author, title, date of publication (in the first reference), and page(s).

14:14), but the devil displays only arrogance, incompetence, and evil, which confirm his guilt.[4]

Human history is the appeal trial of the angelic conflict. The "numerous and diverse aspects of God's wisdom" are revealed through mankind, and most dramatically through the Church, "to the rulers and the authorities [fallen angels] in the heavenly places" (Eph. 3:10; cf., 6:12). As the appeal trial of Satan unfolds, the grace of God and the perfect justice of His verdict are proven again and again. God introduces changes into His administration of human history in order to present His case, disprove Satan's case, and deliver a decisive closing argument. These changes produce the dispensations.[5]

## TIMES AND EPOCHS

Shortly before Christ ascended into heaven, His disciples pressed Him regarding the timing of future events.

> And so when they had come together, they were asking Him, saying, "Lord, is it at this time You are restoring the kingdom to Israel?" He said to them, "It is not for you to know times or epochs which the Father has fixed by His own authority." (Acts 1:6–7, NASB)

The Greek word translated "times" is χρόνος (*chronos*). "Epochs" is καιρός (*kairos*). *Chronos* regards time as a succession of events, one following the other in chronological order. Occasionally *chronos* is used in the Bible for a segment of time and has a dispensational connotation (Rom. 16:25; 1 Pet. 1:20).

In contrast, *kairos* denotes an era, a system or order of chronology, a period of time characterized by a distinctive development. This noun is frequently used for the organization of historical events in their dispensational categories. In various passages *kairos* refers to the Church Age (Rom. 8:18; 11:5; 13:11), the Jewish Age (Eph. 2:11–12), and the "times of the Gentiles," which is not a single dispensation but a broader period encompassing the Church Age and Tribulation (Luke 21:24).

---

4. Thieme, *Christian Integrity* (2000), 173–86.

5. For a description of the angelic conflict in terms of dispensations, see Thieme, *Christian Suffering* (1997), 140–51.

Why were the disciples not told about "the times or epochs"? Actually, they had been told a great deal. Christ had taught them at length concerning dispensations (Matt. 23:27—25:46; John 14—17). Furthermore, the concept of dispensations was already familiar to them: The anticipation of a messianic kingdom of God on earth was part of their Old Testament heritage (Ps. 89:27–29; Isa. 40:3–5; 62:10–12; Micah 4:1–8; 5:2–4; Zech. 9:9–10). It was our Lord's extensive dispensational teaching that prompted their questions (Matt. 5:17; cf., 24:3).

The disciples did not doubt the existence of dispensations. But their idea of the kingdom of God was distorted by anti-Roman sentiment. Like many others in Judea, they resented Roman authority and accepted the popular opinion that the Jews should have political autonomy. Would Jesus expel the Romans? They wanted to know exact dates. They wanted the kingdom now! The political kingdom of God, however, demanded a spiritual response first, which most of the Jews refused to give (Matt. 23:37). Even though the disciples had believed in Christ as Savior, their preconceived ideas about the kingdom of God had kept them from comprehending Christ's teaching. They also had missed the significance of His rejection by Israel and, therefore, had failed to notice a major shift in His message.

Christ presented Himself to the Jews as the Son of David, the King of the Jews, the fulfillment of all God's unconditional covenants with Israel.[6] When Israel refused to accept her rightful King, the promised earthly kingdom of God was postponed until the Millennium, which God will establish at His own perfect time regardless of human acceptance or rejection (1 Thess. 5:1–2). The disciples were still thinking in terms of an immediate Jewish kingdom on earth after Jesus had already shifted His focus temporarily away from the Jews, who had rejected Him, to a new body of believers, the Church. The Church consists of all individuals who believe in Jesus Christ as personal Savior during the Church Age. God is forming the Church to play a special role in the eternal glorification of Christ.[7]

The doctrine of dispensations itself helps to explain why the disciples were perplexed. They were living in a period of momentous events that belonged to neither the Age of Israel nor the Age of the

---

6. See pages 31–34.
7. See pages 64–66.

Church. In the midst of the Dispensation of the Hypostatic disciples failed to notice the end of Christ's ministry to Isr. beginning of His ministry to the approaching Church.[8] Ma. tians today still overlook vital dispensational distinctions and, ֻ ine disciples, keep occupying themselves with issues that are not central to their spiritual growth and relationship with God. Believers who confuse the dispensations cannot clearly understand God's purpose for their lives in the current age (Col. 2:16—3:3).

The arrival of the Church Age enabled our Lord's disciples to comprehend the "times [and] epochs" (John 16:12–15; Acts 1:7). This new dispensation brought a new teaching ministry of God the Holy Spirit and the complete revelation of the doctrines of the Church, which Jesus had introduced.[9] The Church also has a better vantage point from which to see the dispensations. Now the Jewish Age, the Incarnation, and the Church Age can be seen in succession. The Church Age believer has a more complete perspective than Christ's disciples had while He lived in their presence.

The Apostle Paul became the chief advocate of dispensational teaching. Ironically, he was still an unbeliever at the time of Christ's ascension, when the disciples asked their final question. Ultimately, Paul taught dispensations to the disciples themselves (Gal. 2), and through his canonical epistles he continues to communicate to believers in every generation of the Church Age (2 Pet. 3:1–16).

> Our beloved brother Paul, according to the wisdom given
> him, wrote to you, as also in all *his* letters, speaking in
> them of these things [dispensations, in context specifi-
> cally the eschatological dispensations], in which are some
> things hard to understand, which the untaught and un-
> stable distort, as *they do* also the rest of the Scriptures, to
> their own destruction. (2 Pet. 3:15*b*–16, NASB)

At the time of our Lord's ascension, the disciples (including Peter, who later wrote the passage just quoted) had been well taught by the Lord Himself, but they were unstable in the political turmoil of the

---

8. A description of the Dispensation of the Hypostatic Union begins on page 37.

9. These are among the characteristics that set apart the Church Age. See pages 96–97, 131–34.

day, and especially unstable after the shock of Christ's death, burial, and resurrection. Their outlook was impaired by their desire for an immediate kingdom of God on earth. They could not shed this narrow view of dispensations in the final moments before His ascension, and Jesus did not attempt to teach them beyond their capacity to understand. He answered their question only in brief. Time had run out, and a fuller explanation simply was "not for [them] to know" during His sojourn with them on earth (Acts 1:7). The Church Age was coming, whether they realized it or not. Appropriate to the new dispensation, Christ de-emphasized their search for fulfillment of prophecy.[10] He stated only that precise details of timing would not be revealed and left additional revelation concerning dispensations for later. Twenty-one years after Christ's ascension, Paul would describe believers who were oriented to the times and epochs.

> Now as to the times and the epochs [*chronos* and *kairos*], brethren, you have no need of anything to be written to you. For you yourselves know full well that the day of the Lord [His second advent] will come just like a thief in the night. (1 Thess. 5:1–2, NASB)

Paul previously had taught the Thessalonians about that change of dispensations which the disciples had been so eager to see and which is still future today. The exact timing of our Lord's return is not disclosed through Paul or any other writer of Scripture. But a study of Scripture reveals a great deal about the sequence of times and epochs from the beginning of human history to the end. This is the doctrine of dispensations. To know this doctrine "full well" makes the Christian alert to the plan of God for his life.

> But you, brethren, are not in darkness, that the day should overtake you like a thief. (1 Thess. 5:4, NASB)

## AGES AND ADMINISTRATIONS

Besides *chronos* and *kairos*, two other Greek words complete the New Testament vocabulary for dispensations. The noun αἰών (*aion*),

---

10. The Church Age is an era without prophecy. See pages 134–37.

usually translated "age," refers to dispensations as categories of human history, just as in English we say *Age* of Israel or Church *Age* (Rom. 16:25; Eph. 3:9; Col. 1:26).

Perhaps the most descriptive term for dispensations, however, is οἰκονομία (*oikonomia*). Four centuries before the New Testament was written, Xenophon and Plato used *oikonomia* to mean household administration, the authority of parents over their children, the policy and provisions of parents for their children. In the Greek of the New Testament, *oikonomia* had come to mean the management of a household, the administration of a business or estate. *Oikonomia* implies order (rather than chaos), a plan (rather than confusion), an arrangement (rather than disarray). *Oikonomia* itself does not denote time. However, the King James Version translates this ancient word as "dispensation," a term that legitimately has come to connote a period of time, because *oikonomia* describes divine administration during a distinct historical era (1 Cor. 9:17; Eph. 1:8–10; 3:2–3, 8–9; Col. 1:25–29; 1 Tim. 1:3–4). In these passages *oikonomia* identifies the Church Age, during which God administers a set of divine policies and provisions unique to the Church.

Administration becomes an important issue in distinguishing the dispensations from one another. At decisive junctures in His overall plan for mankind, God institutes changes in delegated authority, responsibility, procedure, and available assets. These changes in the divine administration of human history involve first one group of people, then another, and another.

Hence, nomenclature for the dispensations is derived from the people at the focus of divine revelation in a specific period of time. In the march of history, this focus passes from Gentiles to the nation of Israel, from Israel to Jesus Christ in His first advent, from Christ to the Church, from the Church to a besieged remnant of Israel in the Tribulation, and finally from those faithful of Israel to Christ the deliverer, conqueror, and ruler in the Millennium. Each administration involves new divine mandates accompanied by new divine resources for fulfilling those mandates. As a result, the postsalvation way of life for believers may be significantly different in the various eras of human history. Scripture reveals the believer's way of life most comprehensively in the dispensations of Israel and the Church. Less is revealed of God's postsalvation mandates for the other dispensations, but the details that are disclosed confirm the principle of change against a background of continuity.

# DISPENSATIONS AS TAUGHT BY PAUL

Dispensations are not an arbitrary classification superimposed by man on the Bible. They are an integral part of divine revelation. The Greek vocabulary establishes that the subject of dispensations is presented in Scripture. Furthermore, as noted, Jesus Christ affirmed the existence of distinct "times or epochs which the Father has fixed by His own authority" (Acts 1:7).

In presenting the unique characteristics of our own dispensation, the Church Age, Paul repeatedly teaches the doctrine of dispensations. He borrows a Greek term that everyone in his day could understand. Μυστήριον (musterion), "mystery," referred to the secrets of an exclusive religious sect. Numerous mystery cults flourished throughout the ancient Mediterranean world, and although the secrets themselves were closely guarded, everyone knew that these secretive organizations existed. Everyone knew that there were certain rituals, formulas, objects, and rites of the cult of Isis, for example, which were mysteries never revealed to outsiders. Only initiates could learn the 'mystery' doctrines. Paul gave this pagan term a Christian meaning.

The Church was entirely unknown prior to Christ's announcement of the Church Age. Never mentioned in Old Testament prophecy but fully developed in the New Testament epistles, this body of doctrine sets the Church Age apart from the other dispensations. The *mystery doctrine* of the Church unveils the characteristics unique to the Christian way of life. The "mystery" pertains to the Church alone.

Today the English word mystery denotes something incomprehensible, an enigma, or a puzzle. But that is not the meaning of the Greek word. In the ancient world a mystery was *well-known*—although only to the initiated. Likewise, Church Age doctrine should be thoroughly familiar to each Church Age believer. Every Christian is an insider, an initiate, a member of the Church Universal.

Why was mystery doctrine concealed for so long? In the upper room on the night before His crucifixion, Christ prophesied the coming of the Church Age (John 14—17). God gave Him the honor of first revealing Church Age doctrine for several reasons.

First, the Church exists to glorify Him to the maximum (John 16:14; Eph. 1:21–23; 5:25–27). The doctrines of the Church depend on the glorification of Christ (John 7:39), which resulted from His work on the cross. In the hour of His rejection by His people, He unveiled His coming glorification. On the eve of His judgment by the Father, Christ displayed His utter confidence in the Father's plan by announcing its success: the formation of the Church through which God would glorify Him forever (John 13:31–32).

Second, Israel had been given every opportunity to accept the Messiah. Christ revealed the Church only *after* Israel had rejected Him. The Jewish kingdom of God on earth had been postponed until the Millennium, and a new set of options for believers on earth now became pertinent. If revealed sooner, Church Age doctrine would have confused the issue for the Jews.

Third, soon after prophesying the Church, Jesus Christ would become the victor of the cross and resurrection. It was fitting that He be the One to announce the dramatic change of dispensations that His victory would produce. Indeed, His unprecedented prophecy of the Church was one of the most stunning moments in the entire angelic conflict. This announcement was a brilliant, unexpected revelation of God's grace, revealed not only to man but also to Satan and his fallen angels, who constantly observed our Lord (1 Tim. 3:16; 1 Pet. 1:10–12).[11]

Finally, Jesus Christ was personally passing along the dynamics of His own life to be the Christian way of life for the Church (John 13:34; 15:10). Throughout His incarnation He had utilized the system of divine power that the Father had designed to support His humanity. On the eve of His crucifixion, Christ bequeathed this proven system of divine power to every Church Age believer.[12] This power system—the dynamics of the Christian way of life—lies at the heart of mystery doctrine. Church Age doctrine was concealed until the Christian way of life went into effect.

Making reference to the mystery doctrine of the Church Age, two passages of Scripture (with expository notes) illustrate Paul's approach to the subject of dispensations.

---

11. See Thieme, *Victorious Proclamation* (2002), for a second decisive announcement of Christ's victory to angels.

12. See pages 50–52. See also Thieme, *Christian Integrity*, 12–14.

For this reason, I, Paul, a prisoner of Christ Jesus for the sake of you Gentiles [Paul now inserts a parenthetical explanation of the new dispensation that no longer is administered through Israel]—since you have heard about the dispensation of the grace of God [nomenclature for the Church Age, in which God pours out grace more liberally than in any other dispensation] which was given to me for your benefit, that through revelation the mystery [the doctrines of the Church Age, which God revealed only to the Church] was made known to me, as I have already written briefly [as in Romans 16:25–26 and Ephesians 1:9]. By reading this [Ephesians] you ought to be able to understand my technical knowledge about the mystery of Christ [unique and previously unrevealed doctrines of the Church Age] which was not made known to other ages [believers living in the dispensations prior to the Church Age] so that now [for the new dispensation] it has been revealed to His holy apostles and prophets [the apostles to the Church, who recorded the New Testament] by means of the Holy Spirit. (Eph. 3:1–5)

This passage confirms that the doctrine of dispensations is a biblical subject. In a second major passage Paul again presents the doctrine of dispensations by contrasting with all previous ages the special advantages, opportunities, and responsibilities of the Church Age.

Of which [Church] I have become a minister on the basis of this dispensation from God, which has been given to me for your benefit, that I might implement your deficiency of the Word of God, that is, the mystery [Church Age doctrine], which has been hidden from past ages and generations [previous dispensations], but now has been revealed to the saints ["saints" is a technical term for Church Age believers],[13] to whom God has decreed to make known what is the wealth of the glory of this mystery among the Gentiles [in dramatic contrast to the ex-

---

13. See pages 85–93 for a discussion of the baptism of the Holy Spirit, which makes each Church Age believer a "saint."

clusive spiritual position of Jews in the now-suspended Age of Israel] [which mystery is] Christ in you [the indwelling of Christ in every believer, a characteristic unique to the Church Age],[14] the hope of glory [the believer's confidence of fulfilling the plan of God for this dispensation]. (Col. 1:25–27)

God remains the same. The way of salvation remains unchanged. But against a background of immutability and continuity, the doctrines of the mystery reveal the strategic changes that make this new dispensation unique. Church Age believers are a new spiritual species (2 Cor. 5:17) with a totally new position in Christ (Rom. 8:38–39; 1 Cor. 1:2, 30) and a magnificent array of privileges, responsibilities, and opportunities never available to believers of earlier ages (Eph. 1:3–14).

This book will conclude with a survey of the Church's unique advantages. Divine assets currently available, along with the biblical mandates for using them, answer the pressing question, "After salvation, what?" But first the Church Age must be presented in context with the other dispensations so that its uniqueness may be properly understood.

---

14. See pages 128–31.

# Chapter Two

---

# AN OUTLINE OF DISPENSATIONS

## ESTABLISHING A FRAMEWORK

AN OUTLINE WILL INTRODUCE the divine viewpoint of human history. Again, there are three general classifications which include the six dispensations and their subdivisions. After this framework is presented, a descriptive summary of each dispensation will fill in the outline. Most of the dates cited here are approximate.

I.  *THE THEOCENTRIC DISPENSATIONS:* from the creation of Adam to the virgin birth of Christ.
    A.  *The Dispensation of the Gentiles:* from the creation of Adam to the Exodus, Genesis 1—Exodus 11.
        1.  The Age of Positive Volition: from the creation of Adam to the fall of man, Genesis 1:26—3:6.
        2.  The Age of Negative Volition: from the fall of man to Abraham, Genesis 3:7—11:32.
        3.  The Age of the Jewish Patriarchs: from Abraham to the Exodus under Moses, Genesis 12—Exodus 11.

B. *The Dispensation of Israel:* from the Exodus until the birth of Christ; 1441–4 B.C.; Exodus 12—Malachi.
   1. The Theocratic Kingdom: from the Exodus to Samuel; 1441–1020 B.C.
   2. The United Kingdom: from Saul to Rehoboam; 1020–926 B.C.
   3. The Northern Kingdom: from Jeroboam to Hoshea; 926–721 B.C.
   4. The Southern Kingdom: from Rehoboam to Zedekiah; 926–586 B.C.
   5. The Restored Nation of Judah: from Nehemiah to Christ; 516–4 B.C.[15]

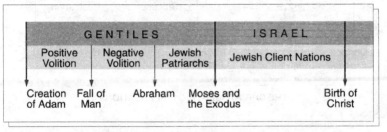

THE THEOCENTRIC DISPENSATIONS

II. *THE CHRISTOCENTRIC DISPENSATIONS:* from the birth of Christ to the yet future resurrection, or Rapture, of the Church.
   A. *The Dispensation of the Hypostatic Union*: the Incarnation or first advent of Jesus Christ and the era of the New Testament Gospels; 4 B.C.—A.D. 30.
   B. *The Church Age:* from A.D. 30 to the resurrection, or Rapture, of the Church.

---

15. Conquered and enslaved, the Jews suffered the Babylonian Captivity (586–516 B.C.) after a long period of unchecked national degeneration and unheeded divine warnings (Jer. 17; cf., Lev. 26). A second period of warnings to Israel extended from approximately 63 B.C. to the destruction of Jerusalem in A.D. 70. The dispersion of Israel is the second administration of maximum divine discipline which continues from A.D. 70 throughout the Church Age and Tribulation until Christ personally restores Israel's client-nation status at His second advent. See page 34.

1. The Precanon Period: the era commencing with the Book of Acts and continuing until John wrote Revelation, completing the canon of Scripture; A.D. 30–96.
2. The Postcanon Period: the current era governed by Christ's Upper Room Discourse (John 14—17), the New Testament epistles, and Revelation 2—3; from A.D. 96 to the Rapture.

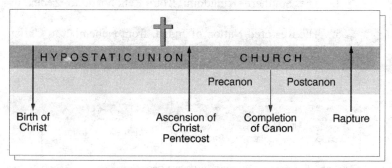

THE CHRISTOCENTRIC DISPENSATIONS

III. *THE ESCHATOLOGICAL DISPENSATIONS:* from the Rapture to the end of human history.
   A. *The Tribulation:* approximately seven years from the Rapture of the Church to the second advent of Christ, prophesied in the Old Testament, Christ's Olivet Discourse (Matthew 24—25), and Revelation 6—19.
      1. Satan's Failed Utopia: from the Rapture until Satan's expulsion from heaven three-and-one-half years into the Tribulation.
      2. The Great Tribulation: from Satan's expulsion until the second advent of Christ.
   B. *The Millennium:* the thousand-year reign of Christ on earth from His second advent to the end of human history, prophesied throughout the Old Testament and in Revelation 20.

*THE ETERNAL STATE* follows the Millennium (Rev. 21—22).

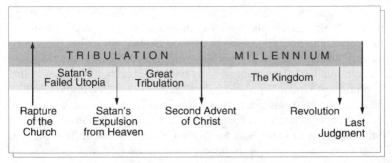

ESCHATOLOGICAL DISPENSATIONS

Throughout this study several descriptive terms will be used interchangeably in discussing dispensations. Epoch, time, age, era, period—these synonyms indicate an extent of time, a segment of history. Interchangeable forms of expression are used as well. The Dispensation of Israel, for example, may be called the Age of Israel or the Jewish Age. And the Dispensation of the Hypostatic Union is also called the Incarnation, the incarnation of Christ, or the first advent of Christ. The particular period under discussion will be apparent from the context (with help from the above outline).

One final point of terminology: The word "Christian" will be used only in connection with the Church Age. Hence, the Christian way of life is the life mandated by God for believers living during the Church Age.

## RESPECT FOR DIVINE DISTINCTIONS

The panorama of dispensations reveals the majestic character of God through the progression and variety of His grace. Each dispensation has a divine purpose, supported by the right divine provisions. The riches of grace available in the Church Age, for example, correlate with God's special objective of glorifying the resurrected Christ to the maximum. This purpose and these provisions explain why the Christian way of life differs from the outpouring of God's grace to believers during other periods of history. The Church Age believer should be eager to understand and use what God has designed specifically for him and thus allow the glory of God to be manifest in his life.

Still, someone might ask, why not regard the Bible as a single whole? Isn't that simpler? Why complicate things with all these distinctions? The primary reason is that the Bible itself makes these divisions. Continuities *and* distinctions established by sovereign God must receive our complete respect, for they reveal something about Him. The unity of God's Word actually is embodied in this doctrine which presents the relationships between the Bible's various parts.

A second reason for recognizing distinctions in the Bible is that the believer needs to know how to conduct his life. As he learns to utilize what God has given to him, he becomes aware of divine policies and assets that are legitimate for other dispensations but that do not directly govern the Christian way of life. When there seem to be contradictions, which commands should he obey? When questions arise, he needs answers. The doctrine of dispensations provides the biblical system of interpretation for understanding why certain divine provisions are currently nonoperational, as well as why others are currently operational.

In no way does this mean the believer can pick and choose which divine commands he wants to obey. Each dispensation is God's administration, not man's, and God gives firm and ample guidance for every period of history. Advancing believers are not disobedient or in danger of lawlessness simply because they do not observe the rules God set forth for another age. Indeed, their spiritual growth comes from *obedience* to God's instructions for the current dispensation. The doctrine of dispensations relieves the Christian's doubts about whether or not God holds him responsible for observing certain practices. This gives his life direction, frees him from a false sense of obligation or guilt, and by answering his questions encourages him to delve deeper into the riches of the Word of God.

The well-informed believer is able to compare and contrast the dispensations. He understands the implications of many statements such as:

> You are not under law [the Mosaic Law, pertinent to Israel],[16] but under grace [the plan of God for the Church]. (Rom. 6:14b, NASB)

> But now that faith [what is believed, the mystery doctrine of the Church] has come, we are no longer under a tutor

---

16. The Mosaic Law is discussed on pages 31–34, 56–57.

> [the Mosaic Law pointing the way to Christ]. (Gal. 3:25, NASB)

> Therefore let no one act as your judge in regard to . . . things [significant in Old Testament ritual] which are a *mere* shadow of what is to come; but the substance belongs to Christ [who set the precedent for the believer's life in the current dispensation]. (Col. 2:16–17, NASB)

The study before us will provide a framework for understanding the Word of God. It also will help protect the Christian from blurring biblical distinctions, from distorting a true doctrinal sense of proportion, and from misapplying divine commands. The doctrine of dispensations teaches what the Christian way of life is—and what it is not.

*Chapter Three*

_____

# THE THEOCENTRIC DISPENSATIONS

## THE AGE OF THE GENTILES

### *Positive Volition*

THE DISPENSATION OF THE GENTILES ENCOMPASSES three subdivisions: the age of positive volition, the age of negative volition, and the age of the Jewish patriarchs.

The age of positive volition involved only two individuals over an indeterminate length of time. Adam and the woman, whose name was אִשָּׁה (*Ishah*), were created perfect in body, soul, and spirit. They lived in perfect environment in the Garden of Eden. They received direct revelation from God when the deity of Christ, who is the revealed member of the Godhead (John 1:1–4; Heb. 1:1–3), walked with them in the evenings (Gen. 3:8). No written canon of Scripture was needed, nor was there need of salvation because man had not yet fallen. The historical record of this period is found in Genesis 1—3:6, written retrospectively by Moses under the inspiration of God the Holy Spirit, who insured the perfect accuracy of the record (1 Pet. 1:21).

This period of positive volition, or perfection, or 'innocence' as it sometimes is called because of the absence of sin, was characterized by two divine institutions: volition and marriage. By planting the tree of the knowledge of good and evil in the middle of the Garden and banning its fruit, God made the volitional issue clear: obedience or disobedience to God.[17] Prece-

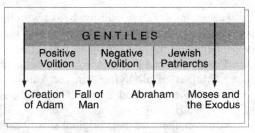

THE AGE OF THE GENTILES

dence in marriage also was lucid. Just as God created Adam the ruler of the world (Gen. 1:26–28; 2:19–20), God also gave him authority over *Ishah* (Gen. 2:18, 20, 23).

The fall of man involved human failure in each divine institution. Both the man and the woman ate the forbidden fruit, violating the volitional issue. By succumbing to Satan, the woman also disregarded the authority of her husband. And the man, in accepting the fruit from the hand of his wife, defaulted in the exercise of his authority over her.

After the Fall, God sustained the institution of volition by holding the man and woman responsible for their own decisions (Gen. 3:11–19). He upheld the institution of marriage by reconfirming the husband's role over the wife (Gen. 3:16). Even with the changes that resulted from the Fall, the perpetuation of the divine institutions is an early example of continuity from one period of biblical history to the next.

Neither human perfection, perfect environment, divine warnings, nor the divine institutions then in effect kept man from the original sin. Human volition is truly free. Furthermore, vital lessons from the age of positive volition still apply to us today, for certain events in the Garden illustrate and illuminate principles found in Church Age doctrine. For example, we see that neither perfect environment nor the

17. Thieme, *The Integrity of God* (1998), 37–44.

ideal marriage can solve man's most basic problems, which are solved
by the grace of God (Phil. 4:11–13; Eph. 5:22–33).

## Negative Volition

The age of negative volition began with the fall of man. Adam and
the woman were now imperfect outside the Garden of Eden. Both
were believers in the Lord Jesus Christ, who revealed Himself as the
Seed of the woman (Gen. 3:15). As a believer, the woman was called
Eve, "Mother of all living," in recognition of woman's role in the
coming of the promised Savior (Gen. 3:20; Isa. 7:14; Matt. 1:20–23;
1 Tim. 2:15a).

At the moment of their original sins, Adam and Eve lost the status
of perfection. They became spiritually dead—separated from God and
totally incapable of a relationship with Him (Gen. 2:17; 3:8). Originally
trichotomous (with body, soul, and spirit), Adam and Eve became dichotomous (only body and soul). Faith in Christ brought regeneration,
which restored the human spirit, making them trichotomous again. The
human spirit has always been essential for a relationship with God
(1 Cor. 2:12–14).

Throughout human history, with the humanity of Christ as the only
exception, every descendant of Adam and Eve is born dichotomous
and remains spiritually dead until he personally believes in Christ
(John 3:18). In all dispensations, everyone who believes in Christ becomes at that moment regenerate and trichotomous, possessing body,
soul, and human spirit (1 Thess. 5:23).

No canon of Scripture existed in the age of negative volition. God
revealed Himself to man through dreams, visions, angelic appearances,
and, as in the Garden of Eden, through direct, physical manifestations
in the form of theophanies (preincarnate appearances of Jesus Christ).
Spiritual authority was vested in the head of the family, who held the
family priesthood.[18] Through this system of authority, God's revealed
truth was communicated to the human race orally and visually in rituals
that included holy days and animal sacrifices (Gen. 3:21; 4:4; 8:20).
The historical record of this period is found in Genesis 3:7—11:32,
again written retrospectively by Moses.

---

18. See pages 29–30, 124–26.

No human missionary agency was required apart from individual believers carrying the Word of God to people in their periphery. The Gospel existed in the form of promises of the coming Messiah (Gen. 3:15), who was depicted in the animal sacrifices: the innocent judged in place of the guilty. Since the fall of man, the means of salvation in every dispensation has always been faith in the Lord Jesus Christ as He is revealed in that era (Rom. 4:1–16; Gal. 3:6–9, 26).

The period of negative volition began with one language, one race, and one culture, but none of these anthropological unities solved problems in human relationships or in man's relationship with God. Furthermore, a third divine institution, the family, was added to volition and marriage. But neither parental authority nor familial bonds nor the family priesthood prevented the first murder, in which Cain killed his brother Abel (Gen. 4:8).

Evil ran rampant during the age of negative volition (Gen. 6:1–7), and God took severe measures to prevent the human race from destroying itself. The universal Flood spared only the family of Noah, the one family of believers that had remained true to God's plan.[19] After the Flood God reiterated His blessing and encouragement, given in the Garden, to "be fruitful and multiply" (Gen. 9:1; cf., 1:28), but with certain changes instituted concerning food (Gen. 9:3; cf., 1:29–30). Here was yet another early instance of change against a background of continuity. From Noah's sons sprang three groups of Gentiles, the descendants of Shem, Ham, and Japheth, which eventually became differentiated nations and races (Gen. 10:32).

Following the Flood yet another evil trend culminated at the tower of Babel (Gen. 11:1–9). There fallen man presumed that he could "reach into heaven" through his own ability and concerted effort. Human achievements often are admirable. They have an evil effect, however, when man's apparent brilliance obscures the reality of his total separation from God or supplants the grace of God as the one real solution to basic human problems. At Babel, therefore, God restrained man's capacity for evil. God had promised after the Flood that never again would He "curse the ground on account of man" (Gen. 8:20–22; 9:8–17), an unalterable covenant that remains in effect through all generations as part of the continuity that runs through all

---

19. Thieme, *Victorious Proclamation.*

the dispensations. True to His own covenant God did not make widespread changes in nature (as at the Fall and in the Flood). This time He dealt with evil by "confusing mankind's language," effectively separating the human race into groups that could not easily communicate with one another (Gen. 11:9).

Thus God established the fourth divine institution: the national entity. He scattered mankind so boundaries between peoples would limit the range of any expression of human arrogance and would impede the spread of evil (Gen. 11:8). Even today, internationalism, or the movement to unify the world under one government, lends itself to evil on a grand scale and opposes the plan of God. Paul's address to the Athenians establishes this principle for the Church Age, allowing Christians to apply this ancient lesson from Babel to the current dispensation. Paul emphasizes that God's purpose in separating the nations and setting "the boundaries of their habitation" is "that they should seek God" rather than be inordinately impressed with the achievements of human genius, which Paul noted in the philosophy, sculpture, and poetry of the Greeks (Acts 17:26–27; cf., 17:21, 23, 28).[20]

## *Jewish Patriarchs*

The age of the Jewish patriarchs was a transitional period from which would emerge the Dispensation of Israel. In this period God founded the Jewish race; in the Age of Israel He would establish the Jewish nation. Although no written Scripture existed, God entered into a covenant, or sworn contract, with Abraham (Heb. 6:13–18), a citizen of the highly cultivated third dynasty of Ur (Gen. 11:31). In a covenant, one party makes a favorable disposition toward another party. God promised unconditionally to "make [Abraham] a great nation." Abraham believed God, and at age seventy-five he obeyed God's instructions to leave his home and migrate "to the land which I will show you" (Gen. 12:1–4; Heb. 11:8–10). The fourth divine institution took on new significance as God prepared to found a particular nation by forming a new race of people. His purpose was not only to constrain evil in the world but also to create a model for the protection of human life, freedom, privacy, and property within a nation's own bor-

---

20. Thieme, *Freedom through Military Victory* (2003), 11–14.

ders. Israel would exemplify the laws of divine establishment. In addition, the spiritual impact of this new race and new nation would continue forever.

Abraham was born a Gentile. He remained so until he reached spiritual maturity at ninety-nine years old. Then with the act of circumcision he became the original Jew, the father of the Jewish race (Gen. 17:1–21). Circumcision was the ritual of confirmation and acknowledgment that the divine covenant required of him. This ritual signified the blessings of restored sexual vigor through which God would "multiply [Abraham's] seed as the stars of the heavens" (Gen. 22:15–18; Rom. 4:17–21; Heb. 11:11–12). Abraham's obedience demonstrated his spiritually mature confidence in God's promises. The Jews were to be a unique demonstration of God's glory among all the nations of the earth.

God confirmed His covenant to Abraham's believing son, Isaac (Gen. 26:3–5), and reconfirmed it to his believing grandson, Jacob (Gen. 28:13–15; 35:11–12). The Jewish race, therefore, is spiritual in origin, descending from Abraham, Isaac, and Jacob, each of whom was a believer in the Messiah, the Lord Jesus Christ (Gen. 15:6). The twelve sons of Jacob are the Jewish patriarchs, the founders of the tribes of Israel.

God's unconditional covenant with Abraham, Isaac, and Jacob is an everlasting covenant. The Jewish race is permanent. Its existence depends on God alone. Israel's eternal heritage is both spiritual and ethnic, just as God promised. He will preserve the regenerate Jewish race and the Jewish nation throughout history and eternity (Gen. 13:15; Rev. 21:12).

Therefore, one of the many blessings that come to the human race through the Jews is a long-term demonstration of God's faithfulness. He committed Himself to specific promises that He will keep through all the vicissitudes of human history. Herein lies encouragement for anyone who trusts in Him. The very existence of the Jews is proof for all to see that God keeps His word. Even when the majority of the Jews themselves reject Him, even when the nation slips into degeneracy, even when He must severely discipline His people, the promise still stands. God never ceases to care for His people. Israel has a future, precisely as God swore to Abraham. In terms of continuity and change, God's covenant with Israel and its literal fulfillment are woven into the fabric of history that remains intact no matter what other dispensations God establishes.

The origin of the Jewish race anticipates an important difference between Israel and the Church. God founded the Jews as a new *racial* species. In contrast, the Church is a "new [*spiritual*] species" (2 Cor. 5:17). Regenerate Jews are God's chosen people and nation, while the Church includes believers of every race and nationality.

The age of the patriarchs ended with the Jews as slaves in Egypt. Moses was born during the age of the patriarchs, but the last forty years of his life belong to the next dispensation, the Age of Israel. Abraham is the father of the Jewish race; Moses, the father of the Jewish nation.

As the population of the earth grew and nations proliferated, God had begun to deal with man in a new way through the covenants that heralded the founding of the nation of Israel. Israel would be God's client nation, His protected representative on earth to whom He would entrust the human authorship and custodianship of written divine revelation.

# THE DISPENSATION OF ISRAEL

## *God's Chosen Nation*

The Jewish Age is related to the *nation* of Israel. The Jews became a nation when God led them out of Egypt, culminating that transitional age of the patriarchs in which He established the Jewish race. As in the age of the Jewish patriarchs, the human race still consisted of a large population divided into many languages, cultures, and nations. As before, all four divine institutions remained in effect, namely, volition, marriage, the family, and the national entity.[21] And as before, salvation throughout the world continued to be by faith in Christ as He was revealed. But with the Exodus, God established one particular nation to represent Him as His missionary agency on earth. The spiritual heritage of Israel continued, as it had begun through the faith of Abraham, Isaac, and Jacob: The Jews expressed their faith toward God as

---

21. Ibid., 5–20.

they offered the Passover lamb. This chosen nation would be given a divine legacy in writing and would manifest God's character as never before in history (Deut. 4:6–8, 32–40).

God chose Israel to be a blessing to the entire human race (Gen. 12:2–3; Amos 9:12; cf., Acts 15:17). He made this nation the recipient, custodian, and communicator of the written canon of Scripture. Not only would Israel furnish the human authors of the Old Testament canon, but the history and function of Israel herself would be recorded forever in Scripture. The God of Israel, who is Jesus Christ, the Second Person of the Trinity (Luke 1:68), personally ruled the theocratic kingdom.

THE AGE OF ISRAEL

There was no division between the spiritual and civil.[22] This was demonstrated to Moses before the Exodus (Ex. 3—4), reiterated to Joshua upon entering the Land (Joshua 5:13–15), and lamented when the apostate people clamored for a human king (1 Sam. 8).

To communicate His grace to mankind through His chosen nation, God gave Moses a code of law for Israel. The Mosaic Law is a remarkable legal system that defined freedom and civil responsibility in Israel for believers and unbelievers alike. The Law also set forth the precise spiritual ceremonies by which the Jews would worship God. Because their God was also their king, it was the responsibility of everyone in Israel to observe the Mosaic Law as part of Jewish national life, although the spiritual provisions were properly meaningful for believers only. As a single, integrated whole, the Mosaic Law focused on the Tabernacle (and later the Temple) where the presence of God resided. Offerings, rituals, and holy day observances conducted there anticipated the day when God would come in the flesh as the promised Messiah. For the orderly conduct of these rituals and for the oral communication of God's written Word, the Law instituted the Levitical priesthood (Deut. 31:9–13; 33:10).

---

22. See pages 60–61, 66–68, 85.

The Mosaic Law was a new phenomenon, a comprehensive system of spiritual ordinances and the laws of divine establishment in Israel under the immediate rule of God. Many of its provisions echo divine commandments given in the Dispensation of the Gentiles when no chosen nation existed. This continuity exists because the ethnic heritage of Israel originated in that preceding age and because divine guidance for each epoch of human history comes from the same unchanging source, God Himself.

I designate the way of life for citizens of Israel as the *ritual plan of God*, in contrast to the *protocol plan of God* for Church Age believers.[23] The rituals prescribed by the Mosaic Law were a dramatic "shadow of what is to come" (Col. 2:17; Heb. 8:5; 10:1). They were types and teaching aids portraying Christ, salvation, and fellowship with God. The Levitical priesthood's function and every individual's daily life included participation in ceremonies that depicted these tremendous doctrines. When Christ later came in the flesh, the reality fulfilled the shadows, making this magnificent heritage of rituals suddenly obsolete (Heb. 8:13). A new code was required, and a new code was provided.[24]

Now in the Church Age the believer's way of life manifests the all-powerful reality rather than the shadow. The ritual plan of God remains part of Scripture, documenting God's faithfulness and describing Christ's Person and work. Therefore, an in-depth study of the Age of Israel, found in Exodus 12 through the book of Malachi, is an essential and highly instructive part of every Christian's knowledge of Bible doctrine.

Israel demonstrated and communicated the grace of God, the greatest expression of which was that she would be the nation through which the Savior would be born into the world. The sequence of promises that guarantee the coming of Christ, beginning with the "Seed" revealed to Adam and Eve (Gen. 3:15) and continuing with the promises made to Noah (Gen. 9:26), became progressively more specific. The Messiah would come from the race of Abraham, Isaac, and Jacob; from the nation of Israel; from the tribe of Judah; from the family of Jesse; from the royal lineage of King David. Since the founding of the Jewish

---

23. A description of the protocol plan of God begins on page 93. See also Thieme, *Levitical Offerings* (1973).
24. See pages 58–59.

race, the promises of the messianic line coincide with the covenants between God and His chosen people.

## Divine Covenants with Israel

The nation of Israel is defined by five divine covenants. The first two covenants, sworn during the age of the patriarchs, prepared the way for founding the nation. God made the remaining three after the Jewish race had become the Jewish nation.

1. *The Abrahamic Covenant* (Gen. 12:1–3; 13:16; 22:15–18; 26:4; 28:14; 35:11; Ex. 6:2–8).
2. *The Palestinian Covenant* (Gen. 13:15; 15:18–21; 26:3–5; 28:13–15; 35:12; Ex. 6:4, 8; Num. 34:1–12; Deut. 30:1–9; Joshua 1:2–4; Jer. 32:36–44; Ezek. 11:16–21; 36:21–38).
3. *The Mosaic Law* (Gen.—Deut.).
   a. Codex I: The Freedom Code (the Decalogue, or Ten Commandments).
   b. Codex II: The Spiritual Code (including a complete, shadow presentation of Christ and His saving work [Christology and soteriology]).
   c. Codex III: The Establishment Code (civil statutes for Israel).
4. *The Davidic Covenant* (2 Sam. 7:8–17; Ps. 89:20–37).
5. *The New Covenant to Israel* (Jer. 31:31–34; cf., Heb. 8:8–12; 10:15–17).

These remarkable covenants are accurately interpreted and most clearly understood in terms of Israel as a nation. They did not and never will belong to Gentiles living throughout the world (Deut. 4:8; Rom. 2:12–14), although Israel was founded to benefit all nations of the earth. Nor did God's covenants with Israel anticipate the Church, which transcends ethnic distinctions and national boundaries, and which in Old Testament times remained an undisclosed mystery (Acts 15:5; Rom. 6:14; Gal. 2:19; Heb. 7:12).

How do these covenants define the nation of Israel? God's covenants to Abraham identify God's elect *people* and the *land* He will give them. Designated the Abrahamic Covenant and the Palestinian (or Real Estate) Covenant, these two divine contracts were the basis for

God's deliverance of the Jews from Egyptian slavery and for the founding of the nation in the promised land (Ex. 6:2–9). The Mosaic Law established *policy* for ethical, spiritual, and civil life within the Old Testament nation. The Davidic Covenant designates the *ruling dynasty* of Israel. And the New Covenant promises *restoration* for the nation under divine discipline and guarantees eventual fulfillment of all unconditional covenants.

## Conditional and Unconditional Covenants

Four of these covenants are unconditional and eternal; one is conditional and temporal. God will execute the Abrahamic, Palestinian, Davidic, and New Covenants to Israel with no conditions attached. He promised to do certain things, and He will. His immutable character guarantees His faithfulness. But since the fulfillment of these covenants will last *forever* (Gen. 13:15; 2 Sam. 7:13, 16; Jer. 31:34), who could be the beneficiaries? Only someone who personally possesses eternal life can be a recipient of eternal blessings. Therefore, the original definition of God's elect people answers this question of beneficiaries: God established the Jews as a *regenerate* race, founded through Abraham, Isaac, and Jacob as *believers* in Christ. Not all Israel is Israel (Rom. 9:6–8). Individuals who were genetically, culturally, or religiously Jews were not party to the unconditional covenants unless they personally believed in the promised Messiah.[25] His Person and work are revealed in the one conditional covenant.

The Mosaic Law alone contains conditional clauses. *If* the Jews would do their part, *then* God would do His part (Ex. 19:3–6; Joshua 1:7–8). The Mosaic Law is a single whole, which can be studied under three categories: Codex I, the freedom code; Codex II, the spiritual code; and Codex III, the establishment code. Codex I protected the Jew's ability to make decisions; Codex II presented the most important decision he faced; Codex III prescribed the environment most conducive to making good decisions.

---

25. Even the unbelieving Jews, who were not a party to the unconditional covenants, are protected under the anti-Semitism clause in Genesis 12:3*a*. This statement of divine approval of pro-Semitism and divine condemnation of anti-Semitism insures the race will survive to enter the Tribulation. See page 34. See also Thieme, *Anti-Semitism* (2004), 14.

The spiritual aspect of the Mosaic Law proclaims the grace of God as the way of salvation and identifies faith as the nonmeritorious manner of entering into the eternal blessings of all the unconditional covenants. Specifically, this codex of the Law presents the Messiah and explains His role as Savior. He is depicted in animal sacrifices, in the precise construction and furnishing of the Tabernacle, in the ceremonial clothing of the Levitical priesthood, and in the rituals that the priests performed.[26] If any Jew believed in Christ, then God not only would grant salvation to that individual but in the same instant would also make him party to the four unconditional covenants.

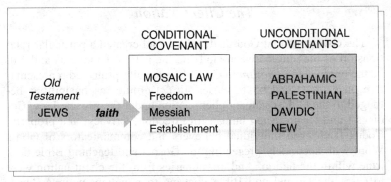

| | CONDITIONAL COVENANT | UNCONDITIONAL COVENANTS |
|---|---|---|
| *Old* *Testament* JEWS *faith* | MOSAIC LAW Freedom Messiah Establishment | ABRAHAMIC PALESTINIAN DAVIDIC NEW |

COVENANTS TO ISRAEL

Moral and civil statutes supported the central spiritual thrust of the Jewish nation. Codex I defined human freedom; Codex III revealed the laws of divine establishment for Jewish government, jurisprudence, military service, economics, diet, hygiene, soil conservation, quarantine, and for every other significant aspect of life in Israel. *If* the citizens of Israel would obey the mandates of Codices I and III, *then* God would temporally bless them as individuals and the nation as a whole (Deut. 28:1–14). With God as its source, this divine covenant far surpassed contemporary systems of national law, such as the overpraised Babylonian Code of Hamurabi.

All divine covenants to Israel will be executed by the Lord Jesus Christ. At present, only the Mosaic Law has been fulfilled completely. In His first advent Christ fulfilled the entire Law, including all three

---

26. Thieme, *Levitical Offerings*, 1–5.

codices, by His sinless life and substitutionary death for the sins of
mankind (Matt. 5:17; Rom. 10:4).[27] In His second advent He will fulfill the Abrahamic, Palestinian, Davidic, and New Covenants when He
returns to earth to restore Israel and rule over her. Even at the peak of
Israel's glory under Solomon, the unconditional covenants were not
fulfilled. Israel has never occupied all of the vast lands granted by the
Palestinian Covenant. But God has not forgotten His people; He will
keep His promises (Gen. 28:14). Both in the Millennium and in eternity, Israel will enjoy a glory she has never yet known.

## The Client Nation

The covenants that God made with Israel created a particular relationship of blessing between God and the nation. Israel was and will
be the unique *client nation* to God, His specially protected representative on earth (Ex. 19:5–6; Hosea 4:6). Definite responsibilities belonged to the Old Testament client nation under the Mosaic Law. Codices I and III protected human life, freedom, privacy, and property.
Codex II charged individual believers and communicators of God's
Word with accurately presenting the Gospel and teaching Bible doctrine within the nation. And missionaries from the client nation were
to carry the Gospel and Bible doctrine to nonclient nations (Deut.
4:6–8; Jonah).

Client-nation Israel was answerable directly to God for the custodianship of His Word. Woe to any outsiders who dared to persecute
the Jews. God committed this protective principle to writing in the
anti-Semitism clause of the Abrahamic Covenant.

> And I will bless those who bless you,
> And the one who curses you I will curse. (Gen. 12:3*a*,
>     NASB)

This solemn clause is part of an unconditional covenant and, therefore,
remains in force to this day. God protects the Jewish race through
every generation of history so that He can ultimately fulfill His covenants with her.

---

27. See pages 56–57.

The privileges enjoyed by client-nation Israel implied responsibility. Not only were the blessings greater, but so was the potential for national divine discipline if Israel refused to obey divine mandates (Lev. 26). Woe to the Jews if they repudiated their trust as God's representatives on earth (Hosea 4:6).

Israel's history is a panorama of successes and failures in relation to her client-nation responsibilities. A series of five Jewish client nations evolved, as presented in the categorical outline of the dispensations.[28] This sequence ended when the long-anticipated Messiah arrived in the flesh.

The virgin birth of Christ marked the beginning of a new dispensation. By the time of our Lord's birth in 4 B.C., Israel no longer functioned as a client nation to God. Instead, she had distorted the Law into a tyranny of religious legalism. Petty, corrupt, and self-righteous, she had lost her spiritual vigor. She could only chafe under the political and military domination of the Roman Empire. This spiritual degeneracy in Israel continued throughout the Dispensation of the Hypostatic Union and extended into the Church Age until finally God placed the nation under maximum discipline in A.D. 70.

Divine discipline to Israel may be traced from 63 B.C. when the Roman general Pompey captured Jerusalem and desecrated the Temple by entering the Holy of Holies. In 54 B.C. Crassus pillaged the Temple. During the Parthian invasion of Palestine in 40 B.C., Herod escaped to Rome and was appointed King of Judea by the Roman Senate. The Jews refused to recognize him as king, but after three years of fighting he captured Jerusalem and purged the Sanhedrin. In 15 B.C. Agrippa visited Palestine on an inspection tour for the Emperor Augustus to insure that Rome's interests were being served. Herod, who was not a Jew, rebuilt the Temple, dedicating it in 10 B.C.

The year in which Christ was born was an unsettling one in Jewish politics. The Pharisees attempted a *coup d'etat*, Herod died in a rage, and his son, Herod Archelaus, became the ethnarch under Rome, inheriting the part of his father's domains that included Samaria, Judea, and Idumea. In A.D. 6, Rome deposed the inept and aggravating Archelaus. Judea was then absorbed into the Roman Empire as part of a third class province with Coponius as its first imperial procurator, or

---

28. See page 17.

governor. The Jews bristled under a succession of procurators, among them Pontius Pilate, whose administration began in A.D. 26.

The Roman province of Judea had long since ceased to function as a client nation to God.[29] Throughout the dispensation of Christ's first advent, from approximately 4 B.C. to A.D. 30, Judea was a dominated nation in spiritual degeneracy. She continued to exist only to make a decision regarding Jesus Christ as Messiah. Having rejected Christ, the spiritually and politically rebellious Jewish state survived for forty years under the principle of grace before judgment. Then, in A.D. 70, four Roman legions destroyed Jerusalem.

---

29. This is corroborated by the divine warning which preceded the destruction of Israel. Her failure as a client nation to believe in the Messiah, to teach true doctrine, and to send missionaries to the Gentiles was dramatized in the first generation of the Church Age. Like a mirror showing the Jews their own apostasy, yet simultaneously revealing God's grace, the spiritual gift of tongues miraculously presented the Gospel to Jews in gentile languages. See pages 69, 91. See also Thieme, *Tongues* (2000), 4–20.

*Chapter Four*

---

# THE CHRISTOCENTRIC DISPENSATIONS

## THE DISPENSATION OF THE HYPOSTATIC UNION

### *Hypostatic Union Defined*

THE SIX DISPENSATIONS FALL into three categories: theocentric, christocentric, and eschatological. We have just described the two theocentric dispensations—the Age of the Gentiles and the Age of Israel—which occurred before Christ came in the flesh. With the virgin birth of Christ, the christocentric ages began. The Dispensation of the Hypostatic Union and the Dispensation of the Church are the hub of human history because of who Christ is and the Church's relationship to Him.

*Hypostatic union* is the theological term for the incarnate Person of Christ, the union of God and man. At the virgin birth, God the Son took upon Himself true humanity and became a new Person—the God-man, the unique Person of the universe (John 1:1–14; Rom. 1:2–4;

Phil. 2:5–11; 1 Tim. 3:16). The Greek word ὑπόστασις (*hupostasis*) means "substantial nature, essence, actual being, reality."[30] Christ unites in Himself the essence of God and the essence of man, forming a new *hupostasis*, a new united essence, called the hypostatic union. In the Person of the incarnate Christ are two natures, divine and human,

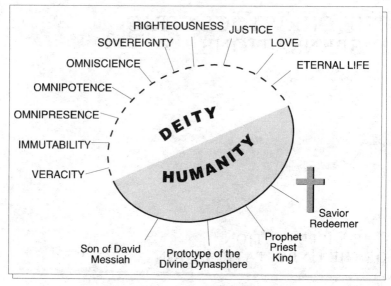

**THE HYPOSTATIC UNION:**
**THE DIVINE AND HUMAN NATURES OF JESUS CHRIST**

inseparably united without loss or mixture of separate identities, without loss or transfer of properties or attributes, the union being personal (the God-man is one Person) and eternal (He will be the God-man forever).[31]

Undiminished deity took upon Himself true humanity in order to be the Savior (Heb. 2:14–15; Phil. 2:7–8), the mediator between God and man (Job 9:2, 32–33; 1 Tim. 2:5–6), the great high priest representing man before God (Heb. 7:4–5, 14, 28; 10:5, 10–14), and the

30. Walter Bauer, William F. Arndt, F. Wilbur Gingrich, *A Greek-English Lexicon of the New Testament and Other Early Christian Literature*, 4th ed., s.v. "*hupostasis*."

31. Thieme, *Christian Integrity*, 210–14.

human King of Israel in fulfillment of the Davidic Covenant (2 Sam. 7:8–16; Ps. 89:20–37). The hypostatic union will continue forever in resurrection body (Heb. 1:8, 12). However, I designate the approximately thirty-three-year period of our Lord's first advent the Dispensation of the Hypostatic Union because this unique period of history began at the resounding moment in which God became the God-man (Heb. 10:5).

The Dispensation of the Hypostatic Union is the epoch recorded in the Gospels, the first four books of the New Testament. This period began with the virgin birth of Christ and terminated with His death, burial, resurrection, ascension, and session at the right hand of the Father in heaven.

THE DISPENSATION OF THE HYPOSTATIC UNION

## Interpreting the Teachings of Christ

Scholars have always found the Gospels exceedingly difficult to interpret. These four books chronicle a unique era in God's plan for human history. The Gospels reveal our Lord's sinless life and saving work, but the record of His earthly ministry also includes His proclamation of the long-awaited kingdom of God in Israel, His prophecy of Israel's future persecution, and finally His announcement of a divine administration significantly different from the Age of Israel. These diverse teachings coalesce in a dispensational framework.

The period of Christ's first advent relates both to Israel and the Church but was itself neither Israel nor Church. In fact, the

Dispensation of the Hypostatic Union *separates* Israel from the Church.[32] Consequently, an accurate interpretation of the Gospels requires an understanding of dispensations.

With absolute authority Jesus Christ presented Himself to Israel as the Son of David, the King of Israel, the Messiah (Matt. 4:17). His presentation took many forms, which Matthew in particular recorded. Christ fulfilled Old Testament prophecy (Matt. 1:5–6; 2:17–18; 4:14–16.). He performed miracles which established His credentials as the Savior of mankind and King of the Jews (Matt. 4:23–25). He announced policy for His kingdom (Matt. 5—7). He explained His identity from Scripture (Matt. 11:25–30; 12:1–8). He described His own death on the cross as the "blood of the covenant [the Mosaic Law]" (Matt. 26:28; cf., Matt. 5:17; Rom. 10:4; Heb. 10:1).[33] In fact, Christ came to fulfill *all five* divine covenants with Israel—conditional and unconditional alike (Matt. 8—9).

Our Lord's sinless life and respect for human freedom fulfilled the commandments in Codex I of the Mosaic Law. His sinlessness and substitutionary death for the sins of mankind were the realities long anticipated by ceremonies in Codex II of the Law. His love for Israel demonstrates His fulfillment of the establishment laws in Codex III (Matt. 22:21). Only He could perfectly execute the entire Law. He came to fulfill every jot and tittle of the Law (Matt. 5:18) whether or not the Jews accepted Him as their king. He made salvation possible, and through His saving work provided entry for the Jews into the unconditional covenants. Any Jew who would believe in Christ as the Messiah became a beneficiary of all the covenants (John 1:12–13).

If enough of the Jews had believed in Christ at that time, He would have executed all the divine covenants with Israel, establishing then and there the promised kingdom of God on earth. But Jewish rejection of the King postponed the Kingdom (Matt. 23:37–39). Christ therefore prophesied the future of Israel in His magnificent Olivet Discourse (Matt. 24—25). In this discourse He painted a vivid picture of Israel's ultimate tribulation and His own return to deliver His people and fulfill the remaining four unconditional covenants in His millennial reign.

---

32. See pages 53–63.
33. Thieme, *The Blood of Christ* (2002).

## *Freedom of Choice under God's Plan*

Jesus Christ stood at a fork in the road of history. He gave human volition an option. He proclaimed that the kingdom of God was "at hand," not that it had actually arrived (Matt. 4:17). In other words, the King was present, but the Kingdom's arrival was contingent on the attitude of Israel. Would the Jews accept or reject their King? We know in hindsight which way history went, but at the time it was an open question. After He offered the kingdom to Israel and purchased salvation for all mankind, what would be the next dispensation? Would the earthly reign of Christ commence, or would some other system of divine administration begin?

Christ presented the kingdom to Israel as a legitimate offer, even though omniscient God knew in advance that Israel would reject Christ as Messiah (Isa. 8:14b–15; Rom. 9:33a). In eternity past God knew that the Church Age would chronologically follow our Lord's first advent. However, God provides real options and opportunities so that man has genuine freedom of choice.[34] God's veracity guarantees that any divine offer is legitimate. God is truth. If He made an 'offer' to the Jews and held them responsible for their decision (Luke 13:34–35) when no genuine option existed, He would be violating His veracity and justice. But God cannot compromise His own nature.

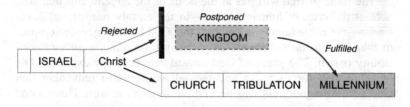

The Gospels seem difficult to understand because they describe a real option presented to Israel, which Israel rejected. But how could Christ have died for sins yet still have established His earthly kingdom at the same time? Christ's death on the cross did not depend on Jewish rejection. The Romans alone could have executed Him, and

---

34. Thieme, *The Integrity of God*, 240–63.

immediately after His resurrection He could have set up His kingdom. This scenario, which in fact the disciples suggested in Acts 1:6, is only one of numerous possibilities. But one is enough to answer the question. Ironically, the nation did reject her king and even played a role in His death. The self-serving antagonism of the Jewish leaders was representative of negative volition in the overwhelming majority of Jewish citizens.

God's plan is never deterred by human negative volition. He remains sovereign while man exercises genuinely free self-determination. By divine decree the sovereignty of God and the free will of man coexist in human history. Sovereign God extends His magnificent grace to man, and the opportunity to accept the grace of God is real in every case. This truth is evident in the Gospel, in which "whoever"— everyone—is invited to believe in Christ for salvation (John 3:16). But many refuse. Man's refusal to accept what God offers and the subsequent continuation of God's plan do not imply that no option existed in the first place. God genuinely offers His grace and desires that everyone accept it (2 Pet. 3:9). But He is never threatened by man's refusal. In fact, human negative volition may elicit extraordinary demonstrations of divine power that glorify Him throughout the earth (Ex. 9:16; Rom. 8:32; 9:17). In the workings of sovereign God even "the wrath of man shall praise [Him]" (Ps. 76:10).

The issue of free will lies at the heart of the angelic conflict. And here at the crux of human history—in the earthly ministry of Jesus Christ—the Bible lucidly documents that God extends genuine options to man. While divine sovereignty remains supreme, man's responsibility is real. The grace of God toward man not only expresses His love but also forces Satan and the fallen angels to remember that God's infinite goodness was poured out to them as well. Human and angelic free will are comparable. Divine grace and human responsibility remind Satan again and again that he bears the full blame for his own revolt against God.

Human history as the appeal trial of the angelic conflict reveals the essence of God.[35] He is gracious, but because He is also sovereign, His plan must go on. Sovereignty implies that His patience toward mankind

---

35. Thieme, *Satan and Demonism* (1996), 2–4.

in delaying judgment and His kindness in granting opportunity after opportunity to accept His grace cannot go on indefinitely. As powerfully illustrated in the first advent of Christ, when Christ turned away from unbelieving Israel and founded the Church, sovereign God *must* ultimately proceed with His perfect plan. Satan and his fallen angels and human unbelievers will ultimately suffer the full and eternal consequences of revolution against sovereign, omnipotent God, while this same God proceeds to bless believers forever in the eternal state.

Given every opportunity to believe in Christ as Savior, the Jews adamantly refused. Certainly there were remarkable exceptions. The disciples, the three Marys, and even Nicodemus show that a remnant of believers can be found in every generation of every dispensation. But the remnant in Israel was too small to counterbalance the vast majority (Matt. 13:10–16).

Israel's rejection of her Messiah does not mean that Jesus Christ's mission on earth ended in failure. He postponed the earthly kingdom of God and initiated a second ministry. As the prophet of the Church, He was the first to announce the mystery doctrine (John 14—17). Thus, in the Upper Room Discourse our Lord unveiled something entirely new: the protocol plan of God for the Church Age. To a degree never before witnessed in human history, the Church Age demonstrates God's magnificent grace and infinite power.

## Accuracy in Interpretation

### DIFFERENT MESSAGES FOR DIFFERENT AUDIENCES

The truth taught by Jesus Christ can apply to believers of any dispensation, but there is a difference between a legitimate *application* from a passage of Scripture and the precise *interpretation* of that passage. There may be many edifying applications that greatly benefit believers in a devotional or practical way, but the objective of rigorous scholarship is a precisely accurate interpretation. Interpretation attempts to discover what the passage means. Each passage must be interpreted in its context in terms of those to whom it is addressed.

Who is the audience to whom Christ speaks in the Gospels? The Gospels can be accurately interpreted only when Christ's ministry to Israel is understood and distinguished from His ministry to the Church.

Several illustrations will emphasize the dispensational orientation required in analyzing the Gospels. In both the Olivet and Upper Room Discourses, Jesus was speaking to the same twelve men, His disciples. He delivered both of these great messages after Israel had rejected Him as Messiah. And both are prophetic. But there are significant differences.

The immediate context of the Olivet Discourse deals with Christ's prediction of the destruction of the Temple in Jerusalem. The Temple was the focal point of Jewish worship, and the disciples, as Jews, were concerned about the promised future of their nation. They asked Christ the same question they would ask Him again just before His ascension: When would He establish His kingdom as the completion and consummation of Jewish history (Matt. 24:3; Acts 1:6)?[36] When would He fulfill God's unconditional covenants with Israel?

At the time of the Olivet Discourse, the disciples knew little if anything about the Church. They may not have known that there would even be an intervening period between the first and second advents of Christ. The Olivet Discourse answers a specific question about *Israel* and guarantees a future for Israel by announcing the Tribulation and the inauguration of the Millennium. The events Christ mentions fulfill Old Testament prophecies of Israel's future (Matt. 24:15, 29–31). They center in Judea (Matt. 24:16). They recognize the Jewish Sabbath (Matt. 24:20b). And they anticipate false applications of the distinctly Jewish hope for the Messiah (Matt. 24:23). In fact, Jesus explicitly declares that the Jewish people will be preserved "until all these things take place" (Matt. 24:34). The context and content of Christ's message point to Israel alone. Therefore, the Olivet Discourse is addressed only to Israel in a context concerning divine discipline against the Jews for rejecting the Messiah (Matt. 23).

In contrast, Christ addressed the Upper Room Discourse to His disciples as the nucleus of the approaching Church Age (John 17:20–21). These same twelve Jewish men were now considered separate from the nation of Israel, which Christ identifies with "the world" that rejected Him (John 13:33–34; 15:18—16:4). In context He anticipated His betrayal and announced His glorification (John 13:31–32). This

---

36. See page 7.

message of His glorification reveals unprecedented assets for the Church Age believer, which will indeed glorify Him to the maximum.

The content of this discourse is new. Nowhere in the entire national heritage of Israel was any believer personally in union with the Messiah, indwelt by Him, or indwelt by the Holy Spirit as described in this final discourse before the cross (John 14:17, 20, 23; 17:21–23, 26). An hour of momentous change had arrived (John 16:1–2, 32). Only the Church was in view.

This sweeping change, fully presented in the New Testament epistles, departs from God's original covenants with Israel. By definition Israel was consecrated and separate from other nations, but now Jews and Gentiles were to be indistinguishable in Christ. God is not contradictory. The conclusion is that Israel was no longer in the spotlight. She had rejected her Messiah. God remained true to His word by not permanently rejecting her, but He was taking the initiative by turning her refusal into an opportunity to demonstrate His grace even more in the Church. As a result, His future entry into His kingdom as the Son of David will be all the greater. In terms of divine administration, God had shifted His historical focus to a new body of believers, the Church.

These two famous prophetic discourses by our Lord differ significantly even though they were presented only two days apart (Matt. 26:1–2). But they perfectly mesh within a dispensational framework. Future Israel, not the Church, must be alert for the triumphant second advent of Christ (Matt. 24:42—25:13). The Church, not Israel, is responsible for utilizing the new outpouring of grace that glorifies the physically absent but indwelling Christ (John 14:13–15; 15:7; 16:23; cf., 14:19–23).

## TEACHING FOR PRESENT AND FUTURE HEARERS

Our Lord's Sermon on the Mount (Matt. 5—7) further illustrates the need for careful interpretation. This was not a private discourse with the twelve disciples, although some of them were present. To whom was this sermon addressed? To Israel? To the Church? To both or neither?

Jesus was speaking to the large crowd of believers gathered around Him on the mountainside (Matt. 5:1; 7:28). His ministry to Israel was underway because He had not yet been rejected by His people (Matt. 12). He was sitting before true, regenerate Israel clarifying the character of God's kingdom and righteousness and contrasting the Mosaic Law's real purpose with the legalism of the Pharisees. Christ was not presenting a way of salvation. His message concerned the believer's postsalvation way of life, which alters from age to age. His teaching differed from the Mosaic Law which was instituted for Israel. The question is, To whom do these instructions pertain?

First of all, the Sermon on the Mount was addressed to the Jewish followers of Jesus who heard Him deliver it.[37] But certain aspects of the message anticipated a future fulfillment—perhaps near future, perhaps distant future, depending on whether or not Israel would accept her King. The hearers realized that all the beatitudes in the opening lines of the sermon had not yet been accomplished even though the Messiah had arrived (Matt. 5:3–11). But if the Messiah spoke these blessings, the listeners could take comfort, fully confident that all *would be* accomplished.

Little did the crowd realize that Christ would be rejected and that the complete fulfillment of His words would not occur in His first advent or in the yet undisclosed Church Age. Even now the meek have not yet "inherited the earth" (Matt. 5:5), nor is God's will "done on earth as it is in heaven" (Matt. 6:10). His will *is* done on earth in the sense that believers can and do accomplish His purpose for their lives, but His will cannot be done "as it is in heaven" until Christ deposes Satan and establishes His own regime. The meek will inherit the earth only under His gracious, all-powerful administration in that future dispensation, the Millennium.

Christ was announcing policy for His kingdom. But He was speaking to His current audience concerning not only the promised kingdom but the immediate present as well, before the kingdom would be established. This is why He needed to mention persecution for righteousness (Matt. 5:12), deliverance from evil (Matt. 5:37, 39), and

---

37. Many Gentiles also were present in the crowd, especially from Syria and Decapolis (Matt. 4:24–25). As in the Old Testament, Gentiles were blessed through Israel (Gen. 12:3) and definitely had access to the kingdom of God promised to the Jews (Ex. 12:38; Zech. 8:22–23; Matt. 8:11). The presence of Gentiles does not change the fact that Christ was addressing Israel.

false prophets (Matt. 7:15). These caveats do not describe the perfect environment of the Millennium. For His then present audience, Christ clarified the believer's way of life at a time when the Mosaic Law was so greatly distorted by the scribes and Pharisees. Such instructions offered encouragement and hope to those who witnessed His earthly ministry yet never saw the reality of His announced blessings. He cared for His hearers in their current state, even while proclaiming the kingdom that He would establish for them if enough of the Jews would accept Him as Messiah.

Christ taught His followers to pray "Thy kingdom come" (Matt. 6:9–13), a prayer which was relevant at a time when sufficient positive volition in Israel would have ushered in the Kingdom. But this petition ceased to be pertinent when in fact that "evil generation" refused Him (Matt. 12:45). Nor will it apply after the Millennium is actually established. Prayer is not needed for what has already come to pass.

Because the Church had not been announced and did not yet exist when Christ spoke on the mountainside, *no* part of our Lord's sermon is addressed specifically to the Church. The correct conclusion is that the Sermon on the Mount belongs to the Dispensation of the Hypostatic Union and to the Millennium, but not to the Church Age.

Church Age believers can learn much from the Sermon on the Mount, however. God is the source of every portion of Scripture, none of which should be ignored as a repository of principles for application. Many points in Christ's message to Israel are also given to Christians. For example, epistles addressed to the Church contain comparable instructions about judging (Rom. 14:10–13; cf., Matt. 7:1–5), logistical grace (1 Pet. 5:7; cf., Matt. 6:25–34), faith-rest (Heb. 4:1–10; cf., Matt. 6:31–34), and the pivot of mature believers, which is the invisible, stabilizing influence within a nation (Eph. 1:21–23; cf., Matt. 5:13–16).

Passages that directly address the Church establish Church Age doctrine. This basic principle of biblical interpretation is derived from the very existence of dispensational distinctions in Scripture. This principle respects those distinctions, balanced by an equal respect for continuities that relate the dispensations to one another. Church Age doctrine is often illuminated by the ways in which God reveals Himself to other audiences in other passages on the same subject. Indeed, when the epistles present a doctrine to the Church, all other biblical passages on that subject must be studied under the principle of comparing Scripture with Scripture.

For example, the Sermon on the Mount offers extensive ethical guidance but with no mention of the ministry of God the Holy Spirit. This does not mean that believers today can exclude the filling of the Spirit from their Christian lives. There are two principal reasons: First, the New Testament epistles command Church Age believers to walk in the Spirit; Second, the Sermon on the Mount was not addressed to the Church, but to believers in an era when the filling of the Spirit was not available. Still, the Sermon's description of the way in which a believer should treat other people sheds light on mandates in the epistles concerning Christian love.

The Olivet and Upper Room Discourses and the Sermon on the Mount illustrate difficulties in interpreting the Gospels that are resolved by the doctrine of dispensations. This doctrine is the biblical hermeneutic[38] that makes the various teachings of Christ lucid. When one understands the different dispensations, one understands to whom His messages pertain. The uniqueness of our Lord's ministry also supports the view that the incarnation of Christ was a separate dispensation.

## The Incarnation as a Separate Dispensation

### FOUR REASONS

The Incarnation, though brief, is a dispensation in itself. The presence of the hypostatic union is too significant to be merely part of another age. From God's overall perspective of human history, something momentous was happening on earth.

At least four approaches lead to the conclusion that these thirty-three years constitute a separate dispensation. First, God revealed Himself to mankind as never before in history—in the Person of Christ. In the Scriptures the life of Christ is recorded four times over, from four perspectives, unlike any other period of history.

---

38. Hermeneutics is the science and principles of interpreting the Bible. See page 2.

Second, God designed the incarnation of Jesus Christ to purchase salvation for all mankind in every dispensation. From God's viewpoint this extraordinary period throws light across all of history and is not hidden away as part of another dispensation. God's design for the incarnation of Christ also included an unprecedented system of power that enabled the humanity of Christ to accomplish His mission.

Third, our Lord's incarnation is a separate dispensation because it plays a major role in defining other dispensations. One of its characteristics—resurrection—becomes a distinguishing mark of the completion of each subsequent dispensation.

And fourth, this approximately thirty-three-year dispensation is like a cornerstone or hinge that connects, yet divides, two very different dispensations. Israel and the Church are different from one another *because* of the Incarnation, which belongs to neither of these dispensations. We will briefly present each of these four approaches.

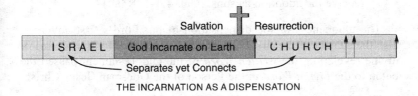

THE INCARNATION AS A DISPENSATION

## GOD REVEALED IN CHRIST

Dramatic change is the opening theme of the book of Hebrews. At the announced place and time, God fulfilled His promises to send the Messiah. Divine revelation now came to mankind in the form of Christ Himself.

> God, after He spoke long ago [in previous dispensations] to the fathers in the prophets in many portions [of the written canon of Scripture] and in many ways [divine communication to the prophets], in these last days [the Dispensation of the Hypostatic Union] has spoken to us

> in His Son . . . [Who] is the flashing forth of His glory
> and the exact representation of His essence. (Heb. 1:1–3)

This long-awaited period of history, called "these last days" in Hebrews 1:2, is also called the dispensation of "the fulness of [the] time." This term is used for each of the two christocentric dispensations, the Age of the Hypostatic Union (Gal. 4:4) and the Church Age (Eph. 1:10), indicating the close relationship between these two dispensations.

> But when the fulness of the time came [a new dispensation], God sent forth His Son, born of a woman, born under the [Mosaic] Law, in order that He might redeem those who were under the Law [by living a sinless life so that He was a qualified substitute to receive divine judgment for man's sins], that we [who believe in Him] might receive the adoption as sons. (Gal. 4:4–5, NASB)

The uniqueness of the dispensation of our Lord's first advent is also the subject of the first chapter of the Gospel of John. In terms of divine revelation, the *written Word* of the Old Testament passed the baton to the *Living Word* in the Person of the God-man, Jesus Christ.

> In the beginning was the Word, and the Word was with God, and the Word was God . . . And the Word became flesh and tabernacled among us, and we beheld His glory, glory as of the uniquely born One from the Father, full of grace and truth . . . No man has seen God at any time; the uniquely born God who is in the bosom of the Father, He has explained Him. (John 1:1, 14, 18)

## THE GREAT POWER EXPERIMENT

God became man and purchased salvation for all mankind of all dispensations—past, present, and future. The incomparable influence of Christ's first advent supports the conclusion that this period is not contained within any other dispensation but must be treated separately and defined in its own terms. During these thirty-three years, the Gospel became an accomplished reality for all dispensations.

The Dispensation of the Hypostatic Union was also distinguished from previous dispensations by the system of power that God the Father designed to sustain the humanity of Christ in accomplishing man's salvation. I have coined a term for this unprecedented sphere of power: the *divine dynasphere*.[39]

According to the Father's plan, Christ did not use the omnipotence of His own deity to support His humanity (Phil. 2:7–8). Instead, God the Holy Spirit constantly empowered and sustained the humanity of Christ amid the hostility of the devil's world (Matt. 4:1; 12:18, 28; Luke 4:1, 14–15, 18; John 3:34; Acts 10:38; Rom. 1:4; Heb. 9:14). In addition to the ministry of the Holy Spirit, the divine dynasphere also included powerful assets for the humanity of Christ to master and utilize by His own human volition. Our Lord used these divine problem-solving devices in executing the salvation plan of the Father.

Because of the divine dynasphere, the period of the incarnation of Christ may be called the *great power experiment of the hypostatic union*. An experiment in this sense is a demonstration of a known truth. The known truth is that the omnipotence of God the Holy Spirit and the perfect efficacy of divine problem-solving devices were fully able to sustain the humanity of Christ. In the power of the divine dynasphere, Christ perfectly fulfilled every demand of the Mosaic Law throughout His life and death. The divine dynasphere proved effective even under the maximum pressure of being judged for all the sins of mankind. The Holy Spirit constantly sustained Him on the cross (Heb. 9:14), and the problem-solving device that I call "sharing the happiness of God" enabled Him to endure the judgment of all human sins (Heb. 12:2).

To anticipate our description of the next dispensation, the great power experiment of the hypostatic union has been extended as the *great power experiment of the Church Age*. Christ bequeathed to every Church Age believer the very system of power that sustained His humanity during the Age of the Hypostatic Union (John 7:37–39; 15:10–11). Our Lord's proven source of power is now available to the Church Age believer for executing the postsalvation plan of God.

---

39. See Thieme, *Christian Integrity*, for a detailed presentation of the divine dynasphere.

The Dispensation of the Hypostatic Union establishes the precedent for the Church Age. Christ lived in the prototype divine dynasphere; the Christian can live in the operational divine dynasphere. The Church Age believer has the privilege of living by the system of divine dynamics under which Christ lived, not by the ritual system of Israel which Christ totally fulfilled and abrogated (Rom. 10:4; Eph. 2:15). We will discuss this precedent later.[40] Obviously, the *known truth* in the Church Age power experiment is that divine power and problem-solving devices are capable of handling any situation that could possibly confront us.

## GIVING DEFINITION TO OTHER DISPENSATIONS

We have noted two reasons for regarding our Lord's incarnation as a separate dispensation. This unique period revealed God in His Son and purchased salvation for people of all dispensations. There is a third reason: The incarnation of Christ helps to identify the other dispensations. This period of time, which is the central focus of human history, and which defines the dispensations, is itself a dispensation.

As already noted, a major purpose of Old Testament Israel was to anticipate the coming Messiah. Israel was custodian of a shadow Christology. Like the shadow of a person that appears around a corner before he does, Israel's spiritual life took its shape from the reality of Christ who had yet to appear on the scene of history. Other dispensations also are patterned after the first advent of Christ. God took upon Himself true humanity to win the victory of the cross, to be the substitute for man's sins. Because God is forming the Church in honor of that victory, the glorified Christ is called the Head of the Church (Eph. 4:15; 5:23; Col. 1:18). Also, Christ became true humanity in order to

---

40. See pages 55–59. Biblical *problem-solving devices* apply at all times but are especially valuable under pressure when clear-cut approaches are urgently needed. Problem-solving devices for Church Age believers include rebound, the filling of the Holy Spirit, faith-rest, grace orientation, doctrinal orientation, a personal sense of destiny, personal love for God, impersonal love for mankind, sharing the happiness of God, and occupation with Christ. All but rebound were used by the humanity of Christ, and for Him occupation with Christ was spiritual self-esteem. These concepts are explained in Thieme, *Christian Suffering* (2002), 10–15; *Freedom through Military Victory,* 69–83. A detailed study of problem-solving devices is presented in audio recordings available without charge as noted on page *iv*.

fulfill the Davidic Covenant to Israel, on which the Millennium is based. Because He will rule in the Millennium, Christ is called the Son of David (Matt. 1:1; 12:23; 22:41–46). Each of these dispensations—the Age of Israel, the Church Age, and the Millennium—is defined in terms of the first advent of Christ.

From another perspective, each dispensation subsequent to the incarnation of Christ terminates with a resurrection. This repetition treats the first advent of Christ as a pattern for dispensations, hence equivalent to a dispensation itself. The resurrection of Christ is the first and, so far, the only resurrection in history (1 Tim. 6:16). Other individuals have come back from the dead, but they were resuscitated, not resurrected (John 11:43–44). Resuscitation restores an individual to his mortal body, but he subsequently dies again (John 12:10). Resurrection gives the believer his resurrection body so that never again will he die (1 Cor. 15:54).

The sequence of resurrections is introduced by the phrase "all shall be made alive, but each in his own order" (1 Cor. 15:22–23). The "orders" are dispensations. The resurrection of believers is dispensational. After this introduction, four phrases correspond to the final four dispensations beginning with the Incarnation. The *Dispensation of the Hypostatic Union* culminated with the resurrection of Christ, the "first fruits of those who are asleep" (1 Cor. 15:20, 23; Rev. 1:5). The *Church Age* will end with the Rapture, or resurrection of the royal family—"those who are Christ's"—who are next in line to receive resurrection bodies (1 Cor. 15:23). The *Tribulation* will conclude with the second advent of Christ—"when He delivers up the kingdom" (1 Cor. 15:24; cf., Rev. 20:4), at which time the Old Testament believers and tribulational martyrs receive resurrection bodies (Job 19:25–26). Finally, this progression of resurrections will culminate with the resurrection of all believers of the *Millennium*—"when He has abolished all rule and all authority and power" of Satan's final revolution (1 Cor. 15:24; cf., Rev. 20:5, 7–10).

## CHRIST THE CORNERSTONE

A biblical analogy illustrates what has been said already about the Incarnation as a separate dispensation. This illustration also depicts the separation of Israel and the Church, a vital truth which gives such importance to realizing that the Incarnation stands as a distinct dispensation between these two ages.

The Bible describes our Lord's relationship to Israel and to the Church in several ways, but one example will suffice in this general study of dispensations. Jesus Christ is frequently described as "the chief cornerstone" (Ps. 118:22; Isa. 28:16; Matt. 21:42; Mark 12:10; Luke 20:17; Acts 4:10–12; 1 Cor. 3:11; 1 Pet. 2:4–7). This expression must be interpreted in light of the times in which it was written.

What was a cornerstone in the ancient world? Two definitions come down to us, one regarding a building's foundation, the other pertaining to structure above the foundation. A cornerstone was a stone laid at one corner of a foundation as the normal starting point for construction. A stone at the intersection of two walls, uniting them, was also called a cornerstone. Both meanings illustrate Christ's relationship with Israel and the Church, although this analogy by itself does not prove the relationship. Christ can be compared to both the foundation and the superstructure in a process of construction. According to this analogy, what is being built? And what is the construction schedule?

As Paul declared to the Athenians, God "does not dwell in temples made with hands" (Acts 17:24). He transcends the "world and all things in it" (Acts 17:25) but has chosen to dwell among men (John 1:14) and in men (John 14:20).[41] Jesus Christ, the God-man, is the foundation for two invisible, spiritual "temples" designed for worship of God throughout eternity. These two figurative buildings are Israel (Acts 4:10–12) and the Church (Matt. 16:18). Each structure is built of individual believers, not of the stone, brick, and timber normally associated with temple construction. This explains why no temple building will exist in heaven (Rev. 21:22). Church Age believers, for instance, are described as "living stones being constructed into a spiritual house for a holy priesthood" (1 Pet. 2:5). This also sheds light on the fact that the Tabernacle in Israel was only a "copy and shadow" of the reality which is in heaven (Heb. 8:1–2, 5).

The two "temples" built of believers will be complete when all members possess resurrection bodies. The Church will become a spiritual temple forever at the moment of the resurrection, or Rapture, of the Church. Israel, on the other hand, will be resurrected in two stages.

---

41. See pages 126–33.

Believers from the Old Testament Age of Israel and believers who die during the Tribulation will be resurrected at Christ's second advent (Job 19:25–26; Rev. 20:4), and millennial believers will be resurrected at the end of the Millennium (Rev. 20:5). With all members in resurrection bodies, Israel will then be a completed spiritual temple forever.

These living temples are built through evangelism and the communication of Bible doctrine. We are "constructed on the foundation [Christ] by means of the apostles and prophets [writers and communicators of Bible doctrine]" (Eph. 2:20). We might speculate that large stones are mature believers whereas small stones are the believers who never learn doctrine, never grow to spiritual adulthood on earth, but who are eternally saved nonetheless.

In contrast to believers who form these temples, unbelievers stumble over the foundation stone (Rom. 9:30–33). The Jewish leaders in the Age of the Hypostatic Union are depicted as builders (Acts 4:10–12), but they rejected Jesus Christ, their foundation. Therefore, work on Israel ceased, postponed until later dispensations (Matt. 21:42–43). In the meantime, construction of the second building, the Church, began upon that same shared foundation stone. The current situation finds the Church under construction while Israel remains a foundation with its superstructure incomplete. The building up of Israel came to a temporary halt while the Church is formed on earth. When the Church is completed, then construction of Israel will resume.

The superstructure aspect of the analogy depicts Christ as the chief cornerstone. He not only connects two walls but divides them as well, separating the Age of Israel from the Age of the Church. As the corner, the Age of the Hypostatic Union ends one wall and sets the standard for another. Israel and the Church share certain features, but one is not merely the continuation of the other. God's administration of human history turns a corner in the life of Christ.

Israel and the Church are separate dispensations even though numerous continuities exist. The way of salvation remains the same in both dispensations, after the pattern of Abraham's faith. God loves both groups of believers, gives them eternal life, watches over them, and illustrates His relationship with each group by an analogy to marriage. Both are elect; both are called to grow up spiritually; both represent God in the world. But fulfillment of divine covenants to Israel is not found in the Church. God does not renege on His promises. Divine covenants guarantee that Israel, as a distinct and permanent nation, will be a blessing forever to all mankind (Gen. 12:3). In contrast, Jews who believe in Christ during the Church Age are included in the Church through the baptism of the Holy Spirit, equal with all gentile believers and not distinct from them (Eph. 2:11–22).

The dispensations of Israel and the Church are separated by the Dispensation of the Hypostatic Union. Israel does not set the precedent for the postsalvation life of the Church Age believer. Christians must "concentrate on Jesus, the prince-ruler, even the One who brings [believers] to the attainment [of spiritual maturity] by means of doctrine" (Heb. 12:2). He is the cornerstone. He, not the Law that governed Israel, is the pattern for the Church Age believer. In the power of the prototype divine dynasphere, Christ fulfilled the Mosaic Law, rendering it obsolete (Rom. 8:2–3; Heb. 8:13; 9:15; 10:9). In the power of the operational divine dynasphere, the Church Age believer advances spiritually and acquires the virtues of the humanity of Christ (Phil. 4:8; 2 Pet. 1:2–4). *Virtue* from executing the protocol plan of God meets and exceeds any demand for *morality* found in the Law (Rom. 8:4).[42]

## The Separation of Israel and the Church

### FULFILLMENT OF THE MOSAIC LAW

The Dispensation of the Hypostatic Union stands as a line of demarcation between Israel and the Church. Christ fulfilled the Mosaic Law on one hand and set the precedent for Church Age protocol on the other. This division is confirmed by numerous passages which state that the Mosaic Law does not define the Christian's way of life (John 1:16–17; Acts 15:5–11, 24; Rom. 6:14; 7:4–6; 2 Cor. 3:7–13; Gal. 2:9; 3:19–25; 5:18; Eph. 2:15; Col. 2:14).

At the Exodus God founded Israel as a theocracy ruled personally by the Second Person of the Trinity.[43] The whole thrust of the Jewish

---

42. Thieme, *Christian Integrity*, 121–49.
43. See page 131.

way of life was spiritual. Because God ruled Israel, every aspect of life in the nation had spiritual significance, and the Mosaic Law did not distinguish between spiritual and secular issues. Obedience to divine establishment was part of the spiritual life of Jewish believers, and observance of holy days and animal sacrifices was required of all citizens, including unbelievers (although these rituals were fully meaningful to believers only). We distinguish the freedom code, the spiritual code, and the establishment code as a categorical approach to communicating the wide scope of the Mosaic Law. But all aspects of the Law add up to one code for a unique political entity with a spiritual origin, a spiritual destiny, and a King who is God Himself.

The Law is an integrated whole (Matt. 5:18; Gal. 5:14). The entire Mosaic Law is a particular expression of God's eternal and holy character (Ex. 19). He gave the Law to a distinctly defined group of people (Ex. 19:3; Lev. 26:46; Rom. 2:17–20; 3:19; 9:4). It was effective for a limited period of time (Gal. 3:23–25). And it was designed for several explicit purposes. The Mosaic Law regulated life in God's unique client nation, exposed man's sinfulness, and demonstrated his need of a Savior, but the primary purpose of the Law was to anticipate the coming of Christ.

> "Do not think that I came to abolish the Law or the Prophets; I did not come to abolish, but to fulfill." (Matt. 5:17, NASB)

The Law was far more than simply a rule of behavior. Although superior to contemporary codes in its moral instruction, the Law was not primarily ethical but messianic. Therein lies its true greatness. Its mandates depicted the Person and work of Christ and protected the line of Christ until He would arrive in the flesh. The centuries-old purpose of the Mosaic Law was achieved by the incarnate Jesus Christ. Anticipation was replaced by reality. This perfect fulfillment is a tribute to the faithfulness of God.

Because all parts of the Law functioned together as one code, the Law has been abrogated as a whole. The entirety of the Law is no longer pertinent and no longer governs any people or nation (Matt. 5:17–19; Rom. 10:4; Gal. 3:23–25; 5:3–4; cf., 5:18; Heb. 8:13; 10:9). The regime of the Mosaic Law has ended. The Church is "not under law, but under grace" (Rom. 6:14).

## THE LAW OF CHRIST

The end of the Mosaic Law does not leave believers or unbelievers lawless (Rom. 6:15; 13:1–7). A new code of divine mandates, which also expresses the essence of God, now defines the believer's way of life. Like the Law, this new code is also an integrated whole. But God's protocol plan for the Church has a different objective: to glorify the victorious Christ to the maximum. The protocol plan accompanies a different array of divine blessings for the believer that are surveyed in the second half of this book. And the protocol plan of God has a different thrust: greater responsibility placed upon each believer to think and apply Bible doctrine for himself in the privacy of his own priesthood. Still, many principles found in the Mosaic Law also appear in the protocol plan. The reason is that both codes come from the same source, from God Himself.

The character of God remains unchanged even as He makes dispensational changes in human history. God was perfect before He gave the Law to Moses, perfect during the tenure of the Law, and perfect when He fulfilled and rescinded the Law in Christ. In fact, the succession of dispensations reveals His changeless essence to man and angels. God expressed His absolute holiness to man in legal terms long before the Mosaic Law existed, and He continues to provide ethical norms and spiritual instruction now that the Law has ceased to govern. Indeed before, during, and after the time in which the Mosaic Law was in effect in Israel, other expressions of divine law functioned among Gentiles to whom the Mosaic Law never applied (Gen. 26:5; Ex. 19:5b; Rom. 2:14–16; 1 Cor. 7:19; 9:20–21).

In the Church Age the operative divine law is not the Mosaic Law but "the law of Christ" (1 Cor. 9:20–21; Gal. 6:2). This also is called "the law of the Spirit of life in Christ Jesus" (Rom. 8:2), which I designate the *protocol plan of God* or life in the divine dynasphere. Christ fulfilled the entire Mosaic Law in the power of the Holy Spirit in the prototype divine dynasphere. The Church Age believer obeys the new "law of Christ" by following His precedent: filled with the Spirit in the operational divine dynasphere (Rom. 8:2–4).

Because Christ fulfilled and abrogated the Mosaic Law (Heb. 8:13; 10:9), practices instituted for the nation of Israel are not included in the postsalvation plan of God for the Church Age. They do not contribute to the Christian way of life. The Church, for example, does not offer animal sacrifices, observe holy days or the Sabbath, maintain the Levitical priesthood, worship in a sacred building, offer tithes, or have minute details of civic life prescribed by spiritual ordinances. There is now a new, universal priesthood of all believers (1 Pet. 2:9; Heb. 7:12; 8:1), a greater emphasis on individual responsibility (Gal. 5:1), and a separation of church and state (Rom. 13:1–7; cf., Matt. 22:15–22).

## TRANSITION BETWEEN DIVINE ADMINISTRATIONS

Three separate dispensations converge in the Age of the Hypostatic Union. This pivotal era is, therefore, a challenge to accurately interpret.

1. *Christ fulfilled* the Old Testament Law and taught His current followers to live apart from legalism.
2. *He proclaimed* His ruling platform for the millennial kingdom.
3. *He unveiled* the plan of God for the Church.

These closely juxtaposed divine administrations—as well as the presence of Christ Himself—exhibit the grace and wisdom of God in unparalleled depth and variety. The period of our Lord's first advent, then, is an extraordinary presentation of God's perfect character.

Each dispensation fulfills its own purpose in the overall plan of God. Although similarities exist, differences in divine mandates distinguish the Incarnation, the Church, and the Millennium, and divine policy for each of these periods differs significantly from the Law given through Moses to Israel. For example, the Sermon on the Mount represented a shift in divine policy. Again and again Jesus declared, "You have heard that it was said [in the Mosaic Law] . . . but *I* say . . . " (Matt. 5:21–48). He proclaimed the kingdom of God to the Jews in terms of their Mosaic frame of reference. He used the Law as the foundation or point of departure for explaining the way of life in the promised kingdom under His personal rule.

Christ also ministered to the current needs of His hearers. Amplifying and clarifying the true meaning of the Law, He taught them how to live free from the legalistic degeneracy that was so pervasive in the nation. Never was the Law intended to be a means of salvation (Matt. 5:20) or a breeding ground for self-righteousness

(Matt. 6:1–18). The Law revealed the necessity for grace and the source of that grace, Jesus Christ Himself.

After Christ was rejected by Israel, He retracted His offer of the kingdom. Instead of continuing to present His kingdom platform, He announced yet a different divine system, the mystery doctrine of the Church Age (John 14—17). In the Millennium the spiritual and the civil will come under one aegis as Christ again reigns, not as God ruling over one nation but as the God-man over both Israel and the entire world. During the Church Age, however, church and state are separate entities. Divine mandates for the Church Age believer cannot be imposed upon the unbeliever, unlike the Mosaic Law which regulated believers and unbelievers in Israel. Rather than institute another legal system that directly governs all people, Christ now controls history in a manner that gives individual Church Age believers tremendous opportunity (and responsibility) for having invisible impact.[44] In the Upper Room Discourse Jesus bequeathed to the Church this new system of dynamics by which He Himself had lived throughout His first advent.

## COMMON PRINCIPLES IN DIFFERENT CODES

The similarities between the Mosaic Law and Church Age protocol reveal God's immutable consistency, but the differences reflect the magnitude of Christ's achievement during His first advent. The utterly superlative quality of His saving work not only is a stated fact of doctrine (Heb. 2:3), but is also indicated by the dispensational changes that followed the victory of the cross and resurrection (John 7:39). Astounding privileges belong to the "new spiritual species" of believers—the Church—who are chosen to glorify His victory forever.

In establishing the way of life for believers of the Church Age, God manifested His character in many individual commands, some of which He had also included in the Mosaic Law. For example, with the full unveiling of mystery doctrine in the New Testament epistles, every one of the Ten Commandments, except Sabbath observance, has also been given to the Church. Even with these similarities, Church Age protocol is not the Mosaic Law. These are entirely different codes, just as the

---

44. See pages 133–39.

United States Constitution is not the same as England's Magna Carta even though they share certain concepts. Continuities between Israel and the Church exist because all divine law reflects the unchangeable essence of God, not because all or part of the Mosaic Law carries over into subsequent dispensations.

Despite numerous continuities, the new policy for the Church Age is not the old Mosaic Law itself. If precepts found in the Mosaic Law pertain to the Church, they do so because they appear in the New Testament epistles, which define the Christian way of life. These common principles belong to the Church because they are part of the "law of Christ," *not* because they belong to the Mosaic Law.

Adherence to divine establishment had a different meaning under the Mosaic Law than it does under God's plan for the Church Age. Because Israel was God's unique client nation, obedience to the establishment aspect of the Mosaic Law was an *integral part* of the spiritual life of Jewish believers. As part of the Law, divine establishment not only preserved the line of the Messiah but also stabilized Jewish society so that over many centuries the Jews would retain the specific national functions that foreshadowed Christ. In the Church Age these special purposes for divine establishment do not exist. The separation of church and state means that the Christian's responsibility to obey establishment is an *application* of his spiritual life rather than an integral part of it. This explains why the Romans considered the early Christians to be deficient in patriotism, not because Christians disobeyed civil law or were irresponsible as citizens but because Christianity did not make civil duty part of one's religion. Again, whereas the Law of Moses pertained to all residents of the nation—believers and unbelievers alike—the "law of Christ" governs believers only.

## THE CONTINUING VALUE OF THE MOSAIC LAW

The Mosaic Law belongs to the Word of God and still has value for the Church Age believer. In Codex I the Ten Commandments define human freedom. Many people assume the Ten Commandments define sin, but this short list of prohibitions does not begin to cover the doctrine of hamartiology. Clearly, these mandates have another purpose. The identified sins destroy the component elements of freedom—which are life, liberty, property, privacy, and divinely delegated authority. In every dispensation believers and unbelievers alike can protect freedom by avoiding these destructive sins. This explains why every provision of the Decalogue, except Sabbath observance, is also found in the "law of Christ."

Codex II presents the purpose for which God gave man free will: to come to a knowledge of Jesus Christ. The ritual provisions of the Law still have value because they reveal the Messiah as the only Savior. In the ceremonies prescribed by Codex II, the sacrificial animal received the judgment due the sinner, portraying forgiveness and personal cleansing. The New Testament reveals that the substitutionary death of Christ on the cross results in forgiveness of presalvation sins when man expresses faith alone in Christ alone (Rom. 5:8–10) and postsalvation sins at the moment of rebound.[45] Fulfilled in the Person of Christ, these details of ceremonial worship in Israel can teach the royal family to appreciate the Lord. The Church Age believer can see Jesus Christ in the Law.[46] New Testament phrases like "the Lamb of God" and "the blood of Christ" dramatically declare that Christ's saving work on the cross is the reality that the Mosaic Law foreshadowed (John 1:29; 1 Pet. 1:18–19).

Codex III contains practical instructions in many fields that were especially pertinent to Israel. For example, agricultural practices or precautions in dealing with disease or sanitation addressed problems that exist throughout human history. The specific provisions of the Mosaic Law may or may not have value in other nations, but they are concrete examples of how establishment concepts apply to particular situations. Above all, these statutes testify to the care and faithfulness of God in guiding His people in specific circumstances that often were difficult.

Many particulars of divine establishment in Codex III of the Mosaic Law are neither reconfirmed nor clearly excluded from Church Age practice. These precepts still reveal the character of God as expressed in governing His client nation, but they do not bear the force of law for any nation but Old Testament Israel. For instance, the principle of capital punishment is given to the Church Age (Matt. 26:52; Rom. 13:4), but its specific application in cases of adultery

---

45. Thieme, *Rebound & Keep Moving!* (1993).
46. Thieme, *The Blood of Christ*; *Levitical Offerings.*

(Lev. 20:10), homosexuality (Lev. 20:13), or juvenile recalcitrance (Lev. 20:9) is not reconfirmed.

God has given the Church Age believer general guidance concerning divine establishment, in contrast to the hundreds of exact laws that precisely defined life in ancient Israel. Each believer has a responsibility to his community and nation, but the separation of church and state during the Church Age entrusts the specific application of establishment principles to each generation. God encourages the Christian to *think* and apply the basic truths of divine establishment according to the legitimate processes of human government in his own nation. Government is "a minister of God to you for good" (Rom. 13:4). An astute political leader in the Church Age who wishes his nation to prosper can learn much from the Mosaic Law without blindly superimposing its exact provisions where they may not apply. Instead, he will adapt establishment principles to the circumstances, objectives, and heritage of his own nation.

Because Jesus Christ fulfilled the Mosaic Law, His Church is free from the Law (Gal. 5:1). Freedom from the Mosaic Law is not lawlessness or lack of direction. Instead, this royal liberty exists within the framework of God's protocol for the Church Age (John 15:10–12; 1 Cor. 9:19–21; Gal. 5:13). The Christian lives under a new law initially announced by Christ and executed in the power of the Holy Spirit (Rom. 8:2–4). Just as the humanity of Christ matured under this powerful system of divine assets (Luke 2:40, 52), Church Age believers also have an extraordinary opportunity to advance spiritually. Among the many continuing uses of the Mosaic Law, this portion of Scripture teaches by contrast that the Church Age is an epoch of spiritual freedom. The advantages of being in union with Christ give believers unprecedented freedom to apply doctrine and grow in the experience of their unique relationship with God.

# THE DISPENSATION OF THE CHURCH

## *The Church in Biblical Perspective*

The Church Age is a brilliant advance in biblical history. For perspective, notice the progress of the dispensations. At the founding of Israel, Moses wrote:

> "Indeed, ask now concerning the former days which were
> before you, since the day that God created man on the
> earth, and *inquire* from one end of the heavens to the
> other. Has *anything* been done like this great thing [estab-
> lishing the nation of Israel], or has *anything* been heard
> like it?" (Deut. 4:32, NASB)

Magnificent though God's client nation was, when the Age of Israel
ended with the advent of Christ, a far greater thing had come to pass.

> God, after He spoke long ago to the fathers in the proph-
> ets in many portions and in many ways, in these last days
> has spoken to us in *His* Son, whom He appointed heir of
> all things, through whom also He made the world. (Heb.
> 1:1–2, NASB)

Following this incomparable revelation of God, the Church still arrived on the scene as an amazing expression of God's power and
grace. The Church is a breathtaking phenomenon. Never before has
the believer held such a position in relation to the Godhead. Scripture
presents the Church as yet another dramatic new departure in human
history.

> "Truly, truly, I say to you, he who believes in Me, the
> works that I do shall he do also; and greater *works* than
> these shall he do; because I go to the Father [the absent
> Christ is represented on earth by many believers over a
> long period, rather than by Himself alone over the brief
> span of the Incarnation]." (John 14:12, NASB)

As a unique body of believers, the Church is united with Christ, imi-
tates Him, glorifies Him, accompanies Him, and will rule with Him
forever. Never before in history have all these privileges been extended to mankind.

## The Epoch of the Royal Family of God

The Church Age began circa A.D. 30 on the day of Pentecost, ten
days after our Lord's ascension, and will terminate with the resurrection, or Rapture, of the Church. An overview of the broad, historical
characteristics of the Church Age will be presented here. Later we will

summarize the privileges of the individual Church Age believer and will discover why the Church Age offers the greatest challenge to the individual believer in all of human history. The Church Age believer's unique status, power system, privileges, and responsibilities will answer the question, "After salvation, what?"

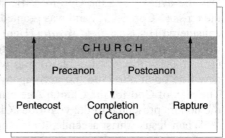

THE DISPENSATION OF THE CHURCH

The Dispensation of the Church is the era of the royal family of God. Every Church Age believer belongs to Christ's royal family, founded as a consequence of His strategic victory at the cross and His rejection by Israel (1 Pet. 2:9). During the Church Age, God is forming this body of believers for the maximum glorification of the Lord Jesus Christ. God gives each Church Age believer the new royal status of the resurrected Christ and extends the great power experiment of the hypostatic union into the great power experiment of the Church Age. The position, assets, and opportunities given to the Church Age believer place the royal family of God in contrast to the family, nation, or kingdom of God in other dispensations.

Christ now holds three titles of royalty, each with a royal family. As God, He has always been *divine royalty* (Rom. 1:4; Heb. 13:8). His first royal title is Son of God, and His royal family includes the other two members of the Trinity—God the Father and God the Holy Spirit. As a man, Jesus became *Jewish royalty* at the virgin birth (Rom. 1:3). His Jewish royal title is Son of David and His royal family is the

| ROYALTY | ROYAL TITLE | ROYAL FAMILY |
|---|---|---|
| Divine | Son of God | God the Father God the Holy Spirit |
| Jewish | Son of David | The Davidic Dynasty |
| Battlefield | King of kings Lord of lords The Bright Morning Star | The Church |

Davidic dynasty. As the God-man, He won the victory over Satan at the cross (1 Cor. 15:57) and was granted a new royal title that may be considered His *battlefield royalty* (Heb. 1:3*b*–4, 13). This third royal title is King of kings and Lord of lords, the Bright Morning Star (1 Tim. 6:15; Rev. 19:16; 22:16). But when the Father conferred this new title upon our Lord, no accompanying royal family yet existed. The plan of God for the Church Age brings to a majestic culmination the honors presented to the victorious Christ.

When Jesus Christ ascended in triumph to heaven (Eph. 4:8), God the Father invested Him with the glories of battlefield royalty and seated Him at the right hand of the throne of God (Ps. 110:1). Then the Father inaugurated the Church Age to establish a royal family for the glorified Lord Jesus Christ. Everyone who believes in Christ during the Church Age is a member of the royal family of God, also known as the Body of Christ or the Church Universal (Gal. 3:28; Eph. 1:22–23).

The very presence of spiritual royalty on earth makes the Church Age unique in human history. During the Church Age every believer can live in the operational divine dynasphere, just as during the Dispensation of the Hypostatic Union the humanity of Christ resided in the prototype divine dynasphere. Every member of the royal family can utilize the divine power and the divine problem-solving devices that enabled the humanity of Christ to win His strategic victory over Satan, sin, and death.

We depend entirely upon Christ. By extending the great power experiment, He equipped us to exploit His strategic victory and win tactical victories in our own lives. As we grow spiritually, the positive influence of spiritual royalty on earth spreads invisibly from the individual believer to other people, to organizations, to nations, to future generations, and to the angels. The personal dynamics of the Christian way of life will be discussed later, but this powerful collective impact of believers is one of the broad, historical characteristics of the Church Age. During this dispensation God maintains a spiritual presence, not a political presence, among mankind.

## Gentile Client Nations

Client nations exist in the Church Age but with a significant difference from the Age of Israel. As before, believers reside in all the nations of the earth, but instead of dealing with mankind through a Jewish client nation, God now works through gentile client nations. He entrusts Christians in these nations with the preservation and communication of the written canon of Scripture. He blesses and protects the gentile client nation as long as the nation upholds its client responsibilities.

Israel is the only nation with which God has sworn an eternal covenant. He will honor His unconditional covenants at the second advent of Christ (Rom. 11:25–29), but Israel is under divine discipline throughout the Church Age and is restricted from her client-nation functions. These are "the times of the Gentiles" (Luke 21:24), which will continue until Christ returns. God now extends client-nation privileges to non-Jewish nations. This divine policy is implied by both Christ and Paul who mandate civic duty toward the Roman Empire (Luke 20:21–25; Rom. 13:1–7).

During the Church Age any gentile nation can serve as a client nation by practicing the following principles:

1. *Protect human life, freedom, privacy, and property* according to the laws of divine establishment;.
2. *Allow evangelism and Bible teaching*;
3. *Serve as a base for missionary activity* to nonclient nations;
4. *Afford a haven of toleration* for the dispersed Jews.

The first principle creates the environment in which the remaining principles can fully operate. The first principle is the chief concern of a nation's government, while the remaining three principles express the spiritual life of the nation's people.

God deals with the client nation in keeping with the spiritual condition of its believers. Blessings to growing believers overflow to the nation; divine discipline of believers who do not advance also affects the nation. This ultimately explains the nation's historical rise or fall (Ps. 34:13–17). Therefore, a thriving client nation that enjoys special divine blessing must maintain a strong pivot of growing and mature believers. Although invisible, the spiritual impact of mature believers residing in a gentile client nation gives the nation its vigor.

The gentile client nation is God's principal missionary agency during the Church Age. As part of the client nation's collective impact, every individual believer as a member of the Church Universal has a personal responsibility to evangelize those in his periphery (Acts 1:8; Rom. 1:14; 1 Cor. 9:16; 2 Cor. 4:5*b*; 2 Tim. 4:5).[47] He is likewise responsible to support the domestic and foreign spread of the Gospel and accurate doctrinal teaching. This support may include prayer, financial contributions, service, or some other form of aid and encouragement.

In sharp contrast to Israel, no specific race of people is elect in the Church Age.[48] Different from the election of Israel, the election of the Church includes every individual believer—Jew *and* Gentile—of any race, culture, or nationality. Strictly speaking, there is no such thing as a 'Christian nation.' The royal family of God on earth exists in every nation, and, unlike the theocracy of Israel, church and state are separate.

This separation is illustrated by the Roman Empire, which was the first gentile client nation. Although Rome was pagan in its official religion, the Church thrived under her protection and toleration during the reigns of the Antonine Caesars (A.D. 96–192). New Testament doctrine never advocates a union of church and state, the interference of Christian organizations into the affairs of state, or the overthrow of pagan government. Rather, government is a blessing (Rom. 13:1–7). Actually, God ordained the benefit to be reciprocal. While the Roman Empire served as "a minister of God to you for good" (Rom. 13:4), the invisible spiritual pivot of mature believers brought divine blessing to the Empire. This unheralded nucleus of Christians existed in the congregations of the Roman province of Asia, located in what is today western Turkey (Ephesians; Colossians; 1 John; 2 John; 3 John; Rev. 2—3).[49]

## Precanon and Postcanon Eras

The Church Age is divided into two categories: the relatively brief precanon period in which the New Testament canon was being formed, and the predominant postcanon period following the completion of the written Word of God. The precanon era is documented in the Book of

---

47. Thieme, *Witnessing* (1992).
48. Election is described on pages 104–09.
49. See pages 137–39.

Acts, which preserves the historical record of the early Church but does not attempt a comprehensive presentation of Church Age doctrines. In fact, certain phenomena found in Acts were required in initiating the Church Age but were no longer pertinent after their purpose was achieved and Church Age doctrines were permanently and authoritatively recorded in the New Testament epistles.

Thus, the precanon period was characterized by temporary spiritual gifts such as apostleship, prophecy, knowledge, tongues, interpretation of tongues, miracles, and healing (1 Cor. 12—14). These temporary gifts were designed to propagate the doctrine of the mystery, to gain a hearing for communicators of this newly revealed doctrine, to organize and administer local churches, and to warn Israel of impending national discipline from God. As these purposes were fulfilled, the temporary gifts were no longer necessary and were gradually removed (1 Cor. 13:8).

Paul, for example, gained credibility with his hearers through the temporary gifts of miracles and healing (Acts 13:8–12; 14:3; 19:11–12), but as his reputation became established, these gifts no longer had a purpose. By A.D. 61 he could not command the healing of even his dear friend Epaphroditus (Phil. 2:27).

Likewise, the temporary gift of tongues was designed to evangelize Jews in gentile languages unknown to the speakers themselves.[50] This miraculous gift was a dramatic sign of Israel's failure as a client nation to carry the truth to gentile nations. Prophesied by Isaiah, the temporary gift of tongues was a warning to Israel of imminent divine discipline (Isa. 28:11; cf., 1 Cor. 14:21). When Jerusalem did indeed fall to the Romans in A.D. 70, the gift of tongues had no further purpose and ceased to exist. The so-called gift of tongues claimed today is an emotional or demonic counterfeit that distracts from Bible doctrine, divides the Church, and debases Christianity. The precanon period came to a close with the death of John, the last apostle, sometime after he wrote Revelation in approximately A.D. 96.

The postcanon period, in which we now live, is the era of permanent spiritual gifts.[51] Gifts like pastor-teacher, evangelism, administration,

---

50. Thieme, *Tongues*.
51. See pages 121–22.

and helps are designed to communicate the doctrines of the written
Word of God and carry out the functions of the local church (Eph.
4:11–13). These gifts sustain the royal family of God on earth and operate throughout all generations of the Church Age.

Gone are the spectacular displays of divine power typical of the
precanon period. Gone are the dramatic rituals and ceremonies of previous dispensations. The postcanon period of the Church Age emphasizes doctrinal *thought* and personal *application* of doctrine. The
Christian lives by divine truth in his own soul rather than depending
on the emotional stimulation of overt rites, divine appearances, direct
revelation from God, or miraculous deeds performed by a few highly
visible Christians. Even in the precanon period the emphasis on doctrine is characteristic of the Church Age (1 Cor. 14:19). The Church is
the most concentrated and sustained presentation of God's grace in all
of human history (Eph. 3:2).

Continual spiritual growth is the believer's objective in every dispensation, but in the Church Age the means to this end are more powerful than in any other age. Mystery doctrine teaches that God gives
each member of the royal family access to divine power in his inner
life (Phil. 3:10) while providing the problem-solving devices designed
originally for the humanity of Christ (John 15:10; 1 John 2:6). Spiritual
victory lies in using these assets. The result is the progressive attainment of spiritual maturity—with all the mental and emotional richness
that maturity brings.

*Chapter Five*

# THE ESCHATOLOGICAL DISPENSATIONS

## THE TRIBULATION

TO REVIEW, THE SIX DISPENSATIONS FORM three categories: theocentric, christocentric, and eschatological. We have just described the two magnificent christocentric dispensations: the Dispensation of the Hypostatic Union and the Church Age. Now we turn our attention to the future.

Eschatology is the biblical study of future or final events. Prophesies yet unfulfilled anticipate history's concluding two dispensations, which are designated the Tribulation and the Millennium. The eschatological dispensations are defined as those after the Resurrection, or Rapture, of the Church. In other words, they will occur after the royal family of God is completely formed and transferred to heaven (Rev. 3:10). The eschatological dispensations are separate from the Church because they are presented in the Old Testament, whereas the Church remained an undisclosed mystery throughout Old Testament times.

For the Jews the Tribulation immediately precedes the founding of God's promised kingdom on earth. Thus, this approximately seven-year period of history (Dan. 9:27; Rev. 11:3; 12:6) is the end of divine discipline against Israel. The Tribulation is prophesied in the Old Testament (Isa. 34:1–6; 63:1–6; Jer. 30:4–8; Ezek. 38—39; Dan. 11:40–45; Zech. 12:1–3; 14:1–2), in our Lord's Olivet Discourse, and in Revelation 6—19. This short, dramatic era will commence immediately after the Rapture of the Church and will terminate with the second

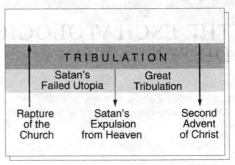

THE TRIBULATION

advent of Christ. It is the "time of Jacob's trouble" (Jer. 30:7) and Daniel's seventieth week (or seventieth seven) based on the famous time-table prophecy of Daniel 9:24–27. The Tribulation might also be called the time of Satan's desperation because of the violent power struggle that will occur (Rev. 12:12).

The first half of the Tribulation will be a time of relative prosperity and overt world peace. Satan will make this one last attempt to establish a 'Millennium' of his own to prove that he is equal with God (Isa. 14:14). But the devil has only his own interests at heart; he cares nothing for mankind but merely wants to use man to prove himself justified in revolting against God. Behind the scenes Satan will be clamping the human race in tyranny through power politics and religious manipulation. Tyranny always flows into the vacuum created by the absence of divine establishment.

Evil will be unrestrained in the Tribulation because the royal family, which is indwelt by the Holy Spirit, will have been removed at the Rapture (2 Thess. 2:7). The outbreak of evil will reveal, through contrast, the historical importance of mature believers as channels for divine blessing. At the beginning of the Tribulation, there will be no believers on earth. The Church's invisible, restraining influence will be gone from the devil's world. In this sudden absence of a spiritual pivot, Satan will have his freest hand. But when Satan is left virtually to his own devices, the world situation will turn grim—characterized by an initial false prosperity that soon deteriorates into horrible disaster. Satan's arrogance will be ultimately revealed in his incompetence. Given every chance, he cannot rule the kingdom he usurped from Adam.

Human failures will multiply under Satan's administration until, through a contagion of bad decisions, a shockingly large portion of the earth's population will destroy itself (Rev. 6:1–11). Except for Eden and the millennial reign of Jesus Christ, utopias are masks for coercion, slavery, and violence. Neither man nor Satan (who is far more capable than man) can create a politically and socially perfect world.

In the middle of the Tribulation, God will eject arrogant, scheming, belligerent Satan from the courtroom of heaven where he has enjoyed free access as defense counsel throughout the appeal trial of the angelic conflict (Rev. 12:7–9; cf., Job 1:6; 2:1; Zech. 3:1). With Satan cast down to earth, the second half of the Tribulation will witness unprecedented violence as Satan's machinations unravel and he desperately struggles to retain his rule over the world.

This latter part of the dispensation is the period actually called the Great Tribulation (Matt. 24:21; Rev. 7:14). Satan will commit all his forces to exterminating the Jews (Rev. 12:17). His purpose will be to eliminate all potential beneficiaries of God's unconditional covenants to Israel. The devil will pursue this heinous policy in an attempt to prove God unfaithful to His promises. Satan will know from Scripture that the fulfillment of God's covenants to Israel is imminent. The Millennium will be only months away. But, reasons Satan, if no regenerate Jew remains alive, God would be unable to keep His promises and fulfill His prophecies. There would be no one to receive the promised blessings. And if God could not fulfill His unconditional covenants (a blasphemous and unthinkable presumption), His character would be flawed, and Satan would have grounds for demanding dismissal of all charges against himself and the fallen angels. But Satan's ploy will not succeed.

In spite of a deceptive peace followed by horrible violence, the Gospel of salvation will be presented more intensively during the Tribulation than in any other dispensation. With the Church removed and with Israel remaining under divine discipline until Christ's second advent, no client nation will be operating on earth. Instead of a client nation, God's principal missionary agency will be 144,000 Jewish evangelists (Rev. 7:4–8). They will risk martyrdom to present the Gospel throughout the world. Supporting and supplementing the function of these evangelists, angels will also join in the presentation of the Gospel (Rev. 14:6–7). Furthermore, two Old Testament prophets— Moses and Elijah—will be resuscitated for a brief but powerful ministry in Jerusalem (Rev. 11:3–13). By all these diverse means, the entire earth will be evangelized thoroughly in the brief span of the Tribulation. Principle: Grace precedes judgment.

An unprecedented world war will break out in the last half of the Tribulation.[52] Watching his utopian kingdom fragment and collapse into chaos, a desperate Satan will set vast human and demonic forces into motion. The ensuing war will culminate in the Armageddon Campaign, in which the forces of four great political powers will converge on Palestine.[53] In Jerusalem a remnant of Jewish believers will refuse to surrender. Brilliantly commanded by aggressive, spiritually mature generals (Zech. 12:5–6), these besieged few will fight for their lives against overwhelming odds. The situation will appear utterly hopeless. The last chance of survival will collapse. Then, suddenly, the Lord Jesus Christ will return to earth and join the battle.

# THE MILLENNIUM

## *The Reign of Christ*

The Lord Jesus Christ will return to deliver the Jews (Isa. 5:26–30; 10:20–23; 11:11–16; 14:1–3; 63:1–6; Joel 2:16—3:21; Zech. 10:6–12). He will come to establish His kingdom in fulfillment of the unconditional covenants to Israel (Dan. 9:24; Zech. 14:9). As King of

---

52. A detailed study of the Book of Revelation is presented in audio recordings available without charge as noted on page *iv*.

53. Thieme, *Anti-Semitism*; *Armageddon* (2002).

kings and Lord of lords, Jesus Christ, the Son of David, will destroy the forces of Satan and depose the devil as the ruler of the earth. The Lamb of God will regather dispersed Israel and rule the earth for one thousand years under the magnificent policies He declared in His Sermon on the Mount. Then will the wonderful prophecy be fulfilled, which describes "many peoples and mighty nations" of Gentiles coming to Jerusalem "to entreat the favor of the Lord" (Zech. 8:22–23).

> "In those days ten men from all the nations of every language [Gentiles] will grasp the garment of a Jew saying, 'Let us go with you, for we have heard that God is with you.'" (Zech. 8:23*b*, NASB)

The Millennium, Latin for "one thousand years," will commence with the second advent of Christ and terminate with the Last Judgment and the destruction of the present universe, including planet Earth. This final dispensation prior to the eternal state is documented in numerous passages of Scripture, with major statements in

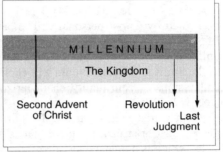

THE MILLENNIUM

Psalm 72; Isaiah 11, 35, 62, 65; Zechariah 14:4–9; and Revelation 20.

When Jesus Christ returns, He will be accompanied by His royal family, the Church, who will reign with Him (Rom. 5:17; Rev. 1:16, 20). Also, the moment of His second advent will mark the resurrection of all Old Testament believers and tribulational martyrs (1 Cor. 15:24). Along with the Church, these Jewish and gentile believers in their resurrection bodies will participate in our Lord's thousand-year reign over the earth (Job 19:25–26).

Following Christ's second advent and His restoration of client-nation Israel, the general outline of the Millennium includes the imprisonment of Satan and his fallen angels (Rev. 20:1–3), the removal of all unbelievers from the earth in the Baptism of Fire (Ezek. 20:34–38 for Jews; Matt. 25:31–46 for Gentiles), and the coronation of Christ. The Millennium will begin with a cadre of believers only, delivered through the Tribulation. In succeeding generations, however, some of their sons and daughters will reject Christ as Savior despite His personal presence and regardless of the wisdom and justice of His rule.

Under the administration of Christ, the earth will enjoy perfect environment (Isa. 35:1–7; 11:6–9; 65:25; Rom. 8:19–21). Universal peace will exist for the first time since the fall of man (Ps. 46:9; Isa. 2:4; Hosea 2:18; Micah 4:3). Prosperity will spread to all nations (Ps. 72:7, 16). Infant mortality will be reduced to zero, and human longevity will increase dramatically (Isa. 65:20). A population explosion will result, repopulating the earth after the decimation of the Tribulation and the divine judgments that initially establish Christ's reign.

Throughout the Millennium there will be universal knowledge of God (Isa. 11:9; Jer. 31:33–34). Israel will rejoice as God's client nation ruled by Christ personally. The believer's postsalvation way of life will again include the filling ministry of God the Holy Spirit, but unlike the Spirit's invisible ministry during the Church Age, the filling of the Spirit in the Millennium will elicit revelatory prophesy, dreams, and visions—a spirituality characterized by ecstatics and emotions (Joel 2:28–29).[54]

With Christ present, the Holy Spirit's ministry of revealing and glorifying Christ can include ecstatics as a genuine spiritual experience, which is not characteristic of the filling of the Holy Spirit in the Church Age. In Christ's absence from the earth during the Church Age, ecstatics would only distract from the true emphasis of the Dispensation of the Church—to demonstrate the sufficiency and tremendous impact of Bible doctrine in the soul of the believer.

In the present dispensation the filling of the Spirit does not elicit prophesy, dreams, or visions, or stimulate emotions. These are not barometers of spirituality. Instead, emotion responds normally to the mentality of the soul, where truth resides as a result of learning Bible doctrine. God set aside the spectacular rituals and miracles of previous dispensations (1 Cor. 1:22a; Heb. 10:1) so that during the

---

54. Ecstatics comes from the Greek word ἐκστασις (ekstasis), meaning "trance" (Acts 10:10; 11:5; 22:17). The trance is an abnormal state of consciousness in which revelatory communication (prophesy, dreams, visions) is received directly to the mentality of the soul from God the Holy Spirit. This revelatory state may include extreme but temporary emotional excitement as a response to the revelation.

postcanon Church Age His manifold wisdom and power are displayed in doctrine—the object of faith—which emphasizes the believer's thoughts and decisions rather than ecstatics and emotions (Rom. 16:17–18; 1 Cor. 1:23–25; Eph. 3:10).[55] In the Millennium, however, the Living Word will be present along with the written Word, sight will complement faith, and under our Lord's control ecstatics can be a genuine spiritual phenomenon on a more widespread basis than in any other dispensation.

## The Conclusion of the Millennium

After one thousand years of perfect environment, Satan will be released from captivity (Rev. 20:7–9). The devil will lead rebellious elements of the human race and his own fallen angels in a desperate conspiracy against our Lord's perfect government. Called the Gog and Magog Revolution, this final outburst of satanic violence will be suppressed immediately. With Satan's argument for the defense reduced to frantic violence and with God's demonstration of grace completed, this will terminate the appeal trial of Satan. Its purpose achieved, human history will end.

At that time all millennial believers will receive their resurrection bodies. This final resurrection of believers will complete the sequence of resurrections, which marks the termination of each dispensation since the Dispensation of the Hypostatic Union (1 Cor. 15:23–24).

At the same time God will resurrect all unbelievers separately from believers (Rev. 20:11–15). The purpose of this resurrection will be to judge all who never accepted salvation. They will be judged not for their sins, for which Christ paid in full, but for rejecting Christ.[56] Unbelievers will be resurrected in one group regardless of the dispensation in which they lived. Here is a final instance of continuity, in contrast to dispensational changes. Unlike the resurrections of Christ and believers in their dispensational order, the common resurrection of unbelievers indicates that salvation by grace through faith alone in Christ alone is the same in every dispensation. All unbelievers alike, of every dispensation, will have refused the same Savior. Presiding in terrible

---

55. Thieme, *Tongues*, 58–59.
56. Thieme, *Slave Market of Sin*, (1994), 20–26.

majesty from the Great White Throne of the Last Judgment, our Lord Jesus Christ will sentence them to join fallen angels in the lake of fire, separated from God forever (Rev. 20:14–15).

Finally will come the destruction of the universe, the creation of a new universe, and the commencement of the eternal state (2 Pet. 3:7, 10–13; Rev. 21—22:5). Mankind will be divided into two categories for eternity: unbelievers and believers (John 3:18, 36). Because they refused to accept Christ as their Savior, unbelievers will remain condemned and will suffer eternal judgment (Rev. 20:15; 21:8). Because of the saving work of Christ, all who believed in Him during their lives on earth will enjoy eternal life in fellowship with God (Rev. 21:3–4; 22:4–5).

*Chapter Six*

# THE UNIQUENESS OF
# THE CHURCH AGE

## CONTINUITY AND CHANGE

GOD HAS A PURPOSE for every believer. What is His plan for you?
After salvation, what?

Dispensations are an essential frame of reference. The biblical answer to "After salvation, what?" lies in the assets God has given specifically to the royal family and in His mandates for utilizing those assets. The Christian way of life is clarified, therefore, by understanding
how the Church Age is unique while being related to the other dispensations. Dispensations orient the believer to God's plan for history.
They unlock the Scriptures for accurate personal application.

Today, many Christians suffer from ignorance of God's plan for the
Church. Some live under the erroneous impression that Christianity is
a blend of the Ten Commandments, the Sermon on the Mount, and a
few contemporary social mores, with no accurate idea of how these

diverse standards coalesce in the doctrine of dispensations. Unable to base their lives on a cohesive understanding of Scripture, many believers exaggerate the place of emotion in worship, a problem which dispensations also help to explain.[57]

Some theologians also integrate Scripture in an unsatisfactory manner. They assume that God's unconditional covenants with the Jews have transferred to the Church and that Israel has become a *spiritual* entity with no national future. They sincerely but incorrectly believe that Israel and the Church are one people, that true "spiritual Israel" is now the Church. But the Old and New Testaments clearly declare that true Israel, the recipient of God's promises, is not only spiritually regenerate but ethnically Jewish.[58] God's magnificent faithfulness to the flesh-and-blood nation of Israel cannot be reduced to a spiritual or a figurative dimension only.

Strong continuity does indeed run through the divine view of history. God perceives all events as one indivisible system, every part of which is essential to the integrity of the whole. But the parts of the whole are still distinct parts. While some theologians look at the whole and see the consistencies, others look at the same whole and see the distinctions. The doctrine of dispensations thoroughly integrates both consistency and distinction, both continuity and change.

Those who think that Israel was merely a foreshadowing of Christ and the Church, or conversely that the Church is a fulfillment of divine covenants with Israel, overemphasize continuity in the plan of God. They underestimate the implications of the changes God has instituted. Striving for an interpretation of the Bible that makes God's plan organic and consistent, they make God's character *in*consistent. Now that the Church exists, these believers wish to dissolve the ethnic definition of Israel and release God from His sworn obligation to honor His promises to His chosen nation. But God *keeps* His promises. He is true to Himself, true to His word, and true to all who trust in Him. Dispensational shifts do not undermine the integrity of God or the stability of His plan. Indeed, these changes achieve His unchanging purpose for human history.[59]

---

57. See pages 69, 91–92.
58. See pages 26–28.
59. See pages 6–7.

Those who give preference to continuity are predisposed to look for correlations among biblical phenomena. They develop their theological systems on their approach to the language of Scripture. The Bible is progressive revelation and is rich in figurative expressions, symbolism, allusion, metaphor, analogy, poetic overtone, and typology. There is continuity in Scripture as the language of the New Testament echoes the Old Testament, but this resonance between the Testaments does not justify the assumption that the people being addressed in the New Testament totally replace those addressed in the Old Testament. When, for example, the Church is called the "seed of Abraham," a comparison is established with Israel. Both Israel and the Church are the regenerate people of God. Both center upon the Person of Christ. But the two are not necessarily the same. Indeed, the differences deserve our respect. The distinction between Israel and the Church profoundly exhibits the character of God. This distinction reveals both His faithfulness to His chosen nation and His justice in answering Israel's refusal by creating an even greater demonstration of grace in the Church. When these truths are glossed over, much of great value is ignored.

On the other hand, theologians who overemphasize distinctions may be too ready to assign concrete definitions and impose rigid structures on the Scriptures. They may remove passages from their full historical context, deny clear comparisons, and ignore important lessons by refusing to admit the value of the entire Bible as a source of applications to Christian experience.

This is not simply a matter of emphasis. It is not a dry, academic argument. The idea that the Church is "spiritual Israel," for example, has harmful implications. It questions God's intention to keep His covenant promises to Israel and, further, casts doubt on the Old Testament believer's ability to understand God's promises. But God does not play with words. God is truth and veracity, and He intends to communicate (Num. 23:19; Ps. 33:4). Also, the organic unification of biblical eras tends to diminish the scriptural emphasis on Church Age doctrine (Eph. 5:32), making believers less appreciative of God's special role for the royal family in the glorification of Christ. To the Christian's enormous disadvantage, the false view muddles the doctrine of the mystery. The blending of Israel and the Church tends to tolerate the legalism of preserving obsolete forms of worship rather

than encouraging among Christians a vigorous love for the truth of
Bible doctrine.

The assertion that the Church is "Israel" also can generate a poten-
tially disastrous political activism as believers work to establish the
kingdom of God on earth. Only Jesus Christ, not fallible Christians
(nor Satan), can bring about the Millennium. Christ will do so in
God's own perfect timing and not according to any human schedule
(Acts 1:6–7; 1 Thess. 5:1–2). This remains the devil's world until the
second advent of Christ, when our Lord will depose Satan. During the
Church Age, believers can live in the confidence that the future rests
in God's powerful hands, as outlined in biblical eschatology, while
turning their primary attention to His plan for glorifying Christ in this
present dispensation.

The plan of God for the Church Age must not be shunted aside by
the fruitless, and arrogant ambition of many Christians to reform or
remake the devil's world. Christians must not instigate or join crusades to whitewash the world. Certainly the Christian is responsible
for being an exemplary citizen under the divine institution of the national entity, but church and state remain separate. Christianity is not
a political movement but a personal relationship with God through
Christ. Whatever may be the participation of believers in their commu-
nities or in the legitimate political processes of their nations, Christians must not neglect their essential calling, which is to attain spiritual maturity. Spiritual maturity itself makes the believer an invisible
hero with a powerful, unheralded, positive impact on his nation and on
human history.

Confusion about dispensations obscures the grace of God expressed in every age, particularly His grace extended to believers of
the current age. As a corrective, therefore, the following survey will
present the characteristics that make the Church Age unique against
the background of trends and consistencies that run through all the
dispensations.

## THE *POLITEUMA* METAPHOR

When a word appears only once in the Bible, we sit up and take
note. Such a word is πολίτευμα (*politeuma*), "the status, rights, and

privileges of citizenship." Paul uses this loaded word in Philippians 3:20. Considering the city of Philippi at the time Paul wrote his epistle, this word creates a brilliant metaphor for the privileges of the Church Age believer. "For our *politeuma*," writes Paul, "is in heaven." The *politeuma* metaphor illustrates advantages that stagger the imagination (Eph. 1:18; 3:20).

A chain of well-known historical events gives tremendous force to Paul's use of the word *politeuma*. The assassination of Julius Caesar on the Ides of March, 44 B.C., rekindled a smoldering civil war in Rome. The renewed conflict would profoundly affect the future of Philippi, a small city in Macedonia.

When Caesar's murderers failed to restore the old Roman Republic, two of them fled Rome to consolidate support in the eastern provinces. Marcus Brutus took over the Roman province of Macedonia, while Gaius Cassius Longinus, the leader of the conspiracy and an experienced general, seized control of the province of Syria. Meanwhile, in opposition to the assassins, Caesar's grandnephew Octavian allied himself with Mark Antony (and Lepidus) to form the Second Triumvirate. Two powerful Roman armies formed—one in Italy, the other in the East. Each numbered nearly one hundred thousand men. A sequence of strategic maneuvers brought these massive forces into contact just west of Philippi.

The Republican army, commanded by Cassius and Brutus, held tactical and strategic advantages over the Triumvirate army of Octavian and Antony. But rashness doomed Cassius and Brutus to decisive defeat. The two battles of Philippi, fought during a rainy three-week period in October of 42 B.C., snuffed out the last hope of the Roman Republic. The victorious Octavian, who would become the unrivaled Emperor Augustus after defeating Mark Antony in a later battle, commemorated the victory by establishing a Roman colony at Philippi. He honored the city as *Colonia Augusta Iulia (Victrix) Philippensium.*

Philippi flourished after the famous victory. A Roman colony was a living extension of Rome herself. A Roman citizen residing in Philippi enjoyed the same status held by a citizen within the walls of Rome. The rights, privileges, and protection guaranteed by Roman law elevated Roman citizens far above their neighbors. Roman citizens in a colony were exempt, for example, from local taxes.

The Bible and many other ancient sources document the superior standing of Roman citizens. Paul was unique among the twelve apostles. He alone was a Roman citizen, and the mere mention of his citizenship brought deferential treatment (Acts 16:27–34; 22:24–29). He was spared beatings, given hearings, and granted access to Caesar himself (Acts 24—26). Even his enemies respected his citizenship. Indeed, so coveted was Roman citizenship that the commander of the Roman garrison in Jerusalem, not a citizen by birth as Paul was, had paid a "large sum of money" to acquire it (Acts 22:28). In Paul's day the Greek term for a privileged colony of Roman citizens, implying the source of all the advantages they enjoyed, was *politeuma*.

The older Greek usage of the word *politeuma* implies privilege and protection for citizens of a powerful state who reside in a distant colony. In 507 B.C., the Athenians defeated the Boeotians and their Chalcidian allies. Athens took possession of the most fertile part of Chalcis, called the Lelantine plain, where the Chalcidian aristocrats had built their estates. To establish Athenian influence in captured territory, the Athenian ruler Cleisthenes divided this beautiful valley into four thousand parcels called κλῆροι (*kleroi*), "lots, portions, or shares," and settled a corresponding number of Athenian citizens there. This was an entirely new concept of colonization. These settlers, or κληρουχία (*klerouchia*), retained all the privileges of Athens although they resided in Chalcis. The body of citizens resident in a foreign country became known as a *politeuma*. Specifically the word came to mean the rights and privileges of their citizenship extended from and protected by their home city-state.

Cleisthenes' Greek system of colonization, as adopted by the Romans, set up the *politeuma* metaphor in Paul's epistle to the Philippians. By Paul's day Philippi was a favorite retirement city for Roman soldiers. Some of the Christians there were probably Roman citizens (Acts 16:27–34). Perhaps some were descendants of veterans of the famous battles. Certainly every Christian in Philippi knew the full significance of *politeuma*. They lived with this system of privilege. Paul's use of this word immediately created a vivid image in the minds of his hearers—an image of highly coveted position and superior opportunity.

We belong to a *politeuma*. We are the nobility of heaven residing on earth.

Roman *politeuma* privileges were impressive, but they only begin to suggest the unfathomable *politeuma* privileges of the royal family of God. Every individual Church Age believer holds the rights and privileges of heaven while living on earth. God has magnificently provisioned us and has thoroughly instructed us so we might "walk worthy of [our] station in life" (Eph. 4:1). The conclusion of this study of dispensations, therefore, is an introduction to the privileges of our heavenly citizenship. Altogether these privileges are unique to the Church Age and determine our Christian way of life.

We will briefly describe ten characteristics.

1. *The baptism of the Holy Spirit.*
2. *The protocol plan of God.*
3. *Mystery doctrine.*
4. *The portfolio of invisible assets.*
5. *The equality factor.*
6. *Royal commissions.*
7. *The indwelling of the Trinity.*
8. *The availability of divine power.*
9. *The absence of prophecy.*
10. *Invisible heroes.*

Some of these *politeuma* privileges require more explanation than others. Some have been mentioned already. A short discussion does not indicate less importance.

All these privileges form a single, balanced whole. Each complements the others. As the believer learns what his assets are and how to use them, they begin to function together as an integrated system. Awareness and consistent use of these assets keep the believer moving forward in the Christian way of life. Indeed, these privileges *constitute* the unique life of meaning, purpose, and definition that God designed for the Church Age.

# THE BAPTISM OF THE HOLY SPIRIT

## *A New Spiritual Species in Christ*

At the moment of salvation, God the Holy Spirit places every Church Age believer into union with Christ (Gal. 3:1–5, 14, 26–27;

Eph. 4:4–5; 2 Thess. 2:13–14). This instantaneous ministry of the
Spirit is called the baptism of the Holy Spirit (1 Cor. 12:13), and it occurs only in the Church Age. "If any man is *in Christ*, he is a new
[spiritual] species" (2 Cor. 5:17, italics added). In this verse the Greek
word καινός (*kainos*) does not mean "new" as in recent, current, or
new in time, like a new coat that replaces an old one of the same type.
*Kainos* means "new" in kind, "new" in species, describing something
remarkable that has never existed before—a totally unprecedented relationship with God (Eph. 1:22–23; 5:22–32). The new spiritual species is the royal family of God.

By placing the Church Age believer "in Christ," the baptism of the
Spirit also links the great power experiment of the hypostatic union
and the great power experiment of the Church Age. In union with
Christ, the believer can utilize the power system designed for the humanity of Christ. In fact, so great is the divine dynasphere that union
with Christ is absolutely a prerequisite for its use.

Jesus Christ prophesied the baptism of the Spirit during the Dispensation of the Hypostatic Union (John 14:20; Acts 1:5). The fulfillment of this prophecy marked the beginning of the Church Age (Acts
2:1–4; cf., 11:15–17). Throughout the Church Age, the baptism of the
Spirit forms the royal family of God, the Church Universal, also called
the Body of Christ.

> For even as the [human] body is one and *yet* has many
> members, and all the members of the body, though
> they are many, are one body, so also is Christ. For by
> one Spirit [God the Holy Spirit performs the action]
> we were all baptized into one body, whether Jews or
> Greeks [Gentiles], whether slaves or free. (1 Cor.
> 12:12–13*a*, NASB)

The baptism of the Holy Spirit sets the Church Age believer apart
from unbelievers *and* apart from believers of all other dispensations.
Every Church Age believer is "sanctified in Christ" (1 Cor. 1:2, 30)
for the "glory of our Lord Jesus Christ" (2 Thess. 2:13–14). The
Greek verb ἁγιάζω (*hagiazo*) means "to set apart, to make holy, to
consecrate, to sanctify." When applied to the Church, sanctification
means that God has created a new species of spiritual royalty, set

apart for the maximum glorification of Jesus Christ: Each believer is in union with the King of kings forever.

## Conformed to the Image of Christ

The doctrine of sanctification teaches that God's purpose is to make each Church Age believer like the humanity of Christ. Each is "conformed to the image of His Son," the glorified Lord Jesus Christ (Rom. 8:29). God accomplishes the Church Age believer's sanctification in three stages: positional, experiential, and ultimate.

*Positional sanctification* is the Church Age believer's union with Christ, accomplished by the baptism of the Holy Spirit. Permanently identified with Christ from the moment of faith in Him, the Christian *retroactively* shares in the victory of our Lord's spiritual death on the cross (Rom. 6:3; Col. 2:12*a*) and *currently* shares His exalted position in heaven "crowned with glory and honor" (Ps. 110:1; Rom. 6:4–5; Col. 2:12*b*; Heb. 1:13; 2:9–11; 10:12).[60]

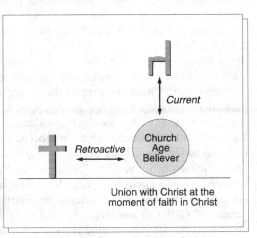

Union with Christ at the
moment of faith in Christ

POSITIONAL SANCTIFICATION

The phrase "in Christ," found throughout the New Testament epistles, is a technical term for the Church Age believer's astounding, absolutely unprecedented union with Christ (John 14:20). In Christ each Church Age believer is positionally superior to all angels, including the chief fallen angel, Satan (Heb. 1:4, 13–14; 2:9–11). This fact of mystery doctrine signals the defeat of Satan, which is why Christ's unexpected announcement of the Church, just prior to the cross, had such

---

60. Thieme, *The Integrity of God*, 93–101; *The Blood of Christ*, 10–13.

a powerful impact on the angels. Also, union with Christ gives equal position and privilege to every Church Age believer, eliminating any basis for prejudice, antagonism, or racial discrimination among Christians (James 1:9–10). Obtained at the moment of salvation, positional sanctification defines the nature of the Christian's way of life *after* salvation as he walks "in newness of life" (Rom. 6:4).

*Experiential sanctification* is residence, function, and spiritual momentum in the divine dynasphere during the believer's life on earth. Living in the divine dynasphere, which the Holy Spirit energizes, fulfills the protocol plan of God (John 17:17; 2 Tim. 2:21; Heb. 9:13–14).

Because we are in union with Christ, we now are able to be sustained, nourished, and empowered by the postsalvation ministry of the Spirit (John 7:37–39; 14:15–17; 16:13–14). Thus we become "partakers of the divine nature" in experience just as we are in position (2 Pet. 1:4). The Holy Spirit's postsalvation ministry is called the filling of the Spirit (Eph. 5:18), which enables us to "walk by means of the Spirit" (Gal. 5:16) in a manner "worthy of [our] station in life" (Eph. 4:1).[61]

United with Christ and granted the same power system in which His humanity constantly lived, we are equipped to be "imitators of God . . . and [to] walk . . . just as Christ [walked]" (Eph. 5:1–2; Gal. 5:16; 1 John 2:6). He functioned in the prototype divine dynasphere; we can function in the operational divine dynasphere (John 14:11–12). In the divine dynasphere we live "through the Spirit, by faith [what is believed—Bible doctrine]" (Gal. 5:5). The mind of Christ, or Bible doctrine in the soul, is the material the Spirit uses to manufacture the virtues of Christ in our lives (Rom. 13:14). In a different metaphor, doctrine is the nutrient that the Holy Spirit uses to produce the "fruit of the Spirit" (Gal. 5:22–23).

Therefore, experiential sanctification has both absolute and progressive aspects. The filling of the Spirit is an *absolute* status. At any given time, the believer is either 100 percent filled with the Spirit or he is not filled with the Spirit at all. Either he is in fellowship with God, or he is out of fellowship. If he has confessed his sins to God, the believer is entirely inside the divine dynasphere (1 John 1:9), but when he sins, and as long as he does not confess to God, he is entirely outside the divine dynasphere. Outside the divine dynasphere

---

61. Thieme, *Old Sin Nature vs. Holy Spirit* (2000).

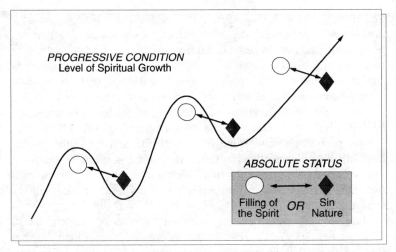

PROGRESSIVE CONDITION
Level of Spiritual Growth

ABSOLUTE STATUS

Filling of the Spirit OR Sin Nature

EXPERIENTIAL SANCTIFICATION

he "grieves" or "quenches" the Holy Spirit (Eph. 4:30; 1 Thess. 5:19) and resides instead in Satan's cosmic system.[62]

This absolute but invisible status—in or out—has a cumulative effect, which is the *progressive* aspect of experiential sanctification. The power of the divine dynasphere is essential for spiritual growth. Only in the divine dynasphere can the believer learn Bible doctrine or accurately apply spiritual truth. What is the dominant trend of his decisions at any given time? Has he been consistently obedient to God's mandates that comprise the divine dynasphere, or has he neglected these divine commands? Is he more often in or out of fellowship with God? Spiritual growth comes from consistency, and as the believer grows, this consistency in executing God's protocol plan becomes a stronger and stronger impetus in his life. Every day he learns and applies doctrine; his inner person is renewed day by day (2 Cor. 4:16). His thinking is renovated according to the pattern of divine thinking in Bible doctrine (Rom. 12:2; Eph. 4:23). He gradually acquires the virtues of Christ.

As growth continues, the filling of the Spirit produces more of the fruit of the Spirit whenever the believer is in the divine dynasphere.

---

62. Thieme, *Christian Integrity*, 173–82.

For example, a novice believer can be just as filled with the Spirit as the mature believer. But the mature believer understands a great deal more Bible doctrine. When the mature Christian is filled with the Spirit, he manifests the "newness of life" more than the beginner who equally is filled with the Spirit but understands less doctrine. A greater understanding and application of doctrine in the believer's thinking causes greater manifestations of the filling of the Spirit in the believer's life. Add to this the fact that as a Christian grows, he spends a greater proportion of his time filled with the Spirit. In other words, both quantity and quality improve: More time is spent in the divine dynasphere with a greater depth of doctrinal resources for the Spirit to use. This explains the increasing effect of divine dynamics within a Christian's life.

Experiential sanctification is called "godliness" (1 Tim. 3:16; 4:7–8; 2 Pet. 1:3; 3:11). True godliness runs far deeper than the shallow legalisms that so many Christians practice. Genuine godliness is abiding in the sphere of Christ's love, which He equated with obedience to His commandments (John 15:10; Eph. 5:2). The sphere of Christ's love *is* the divine dynasphere. The commandments of the Christian way of life coalesce as one consistent system, a single complex of interrelated and mutually supporting elements, an integrated sphere of divine power. This divine system of love and power is the place of godliness. The Christian way of life is life in the divine dynasphere. Here, in principle, is the answer to the question, "After salvation, what?"

Experiential sanctification is potential for the believer, commanded but not guaranteed. God provides the resources, opportunities, instructions, encouragement, and even the divine discipline, but the believer himself chooses to execute the protocol plan of God or not. Volition remains a central issue in the Church Age, as in every dispensation throughout the angelic conflict. But God's faithfulness is also a consistent theme. The believer's failure to live by the mandates of experiential sanctification never cancels positional or ultimate sanctification, which *are* guaranteed by the very essence of God (2 Tim. 2:13).

After our postsalvation lives on earth have ended, God will achieve our *ultimate sanctification* at the resurrection, or Rapture, of the Church. In that future moment He will provide the resurrection body, making us physically like Christ (1 Cor. 1:8; Eph. 1:4; Phil. 3:21; 1 Thess. 5:23; 1 John 3:2).

## Misconceptions of the Baptism of the Spirit

The doctrine of the baptism of the Holy Spirit is widely distorted today. We must state what the baptism of the Spirit is *not*. The baptism of the Spirit is not the same as the filling of the Spirit, as just noted. The baptism of the Holy Spirit also is not an experience or a 'second work of grace' after salvation. It is not, and never was, speaking in tongues.[63]

The idea that Spirit baptism involves speaking in tongues fails to distinguish the doctrine of the baptism of the Holy Spirit from the doctrine of spiritual gifts. The baptism of the Spirit occurs at the instant of salvation for all Church Age believers; the gift of tongues formerly operated only in the postsalvation experience of a few first-century Christians. The phenomenon of tongues was a temporary spiritual gift designed, as Isaiah prophesied, to warn Israel of impending national judgment (Isa. 28:11; 1 Cor. 14:21–22*a*). Jews were evangelized in gentile languages understood by the listeners but not the speakers. This ironic gift exercised by certain early Christians dramatized the Jews' failure to evangelize the Gentiles. Because the gift of tongues was a miraculous sign to alert Israel to her decadence, no one has legitimately spoken in tongues since A.D. 70 when Jerusalem fell, the Jews were dispersed, and the purpose for this temporary gift expired.

> If *there are* tongues, they will cease. (1 Cor. 13:8*b*, NASB)

The dramatic gift of tongues ceased long ago, but the baptism of the Spirit occurs in every generation of the Church Age. And never does this instantaneous work of the Spirit involve ecstatics or emotion. Indeed, the baptism of the Holy Spirit has absolutely no relation to feelings. The believer may be elated or feel nothing at the moment of salvation. He may even feel horrible, but regardless of how he feels, in

---

63. Thieme, *Tongues*, 30–36.

that initial instant of faith in Christ, the Holy Spirit unites him with Christ.

No one senses or detects the baptism of the Spirit in any way. Neither sight, hearing, smell, taste, nor touch confirms this doctrine. Nor does any so-called sixth sense or intuition. The Spirit's ministry at salvation is known only through Bible doctrine, which the believer learns *after* salvation.

The baptism of the Spirit is never earned nor deserved by the believer. God gives this fabulous gift by grace, totally without regard for human merit or human works. Union with Christ is complete at the instant of salvation, accomplished entirely by the grace of God before any believer has a chance to achieve spiritual growth, perform any Christian service, or even learn about these things. The baptism of the Spirit is not progressive and cannot be improved. Furthermore, this instantaneous work of God the Holy Spirit for every Church Age believer is permanent. Never in all eternity can it be undone, lost, or canceled, and never does it need to be repeated (Rom. 8:38–39).

## Sharing All Christ Has and Is

As the mechanics of positional sanctification, the baptism of the Holy Spirit causes the Christian to share in all Christ has and is. Every member of the royal family of God shares Christ's election (Eph. 1:4), His destiny (Rom. 8:28, 30; Eph. 1:5), His sonship (Gal. 3:26; 1 John 3:1–2), His heirship (Rom. 8:16–17), His priesthood (Heb. 10:10–14; 1 Pet. 2:9), His sanctification (1 Cor. 1:2, 30), His royalty (2 Pet. 1:11), His righteousness (2 Cor. 5:21), and His eternal life (1 John 5:11–12).

Divine righteousness and eternal life are necessary for a relationship with God. To live with *perfect* God *forever*, man needs God's own righteousness and God's own life. These blessings, therefore, are inherent in salvation in every dispensation. Old Testament believers were given the righteousness of God and eternal life through imputation rather than through union with Christ (Gen. 15:6; Ps. 23:6). In the Church Age every believer receives divine righteousness and eternal life by imputation *and* by union with Christ (2 Cor. 5:21; 1 John 5:11). This double portion belongs to spiritual royalty alone.[64]

---

64. Thieme, *The Integrity of God*, 74–114.

One vivid description of the baptism of the Holy Spirit contrasts the Church and Israel. To teach the Church Age believer's position in Christ, Paul draws an analogy to the custom of "adoption" practiced by the Roman aristocracy. Roman adoption officially designated someone as an heir, whether or not that person was related by blood. The Caesars usually adopted successors who were not their sons. Often, however, a father would adopt his own son, granting him the full privileges and responsibilities of the family name. The ceremony also marked the boy's transition into adulthood, traditionally at age fourteen. Paul depicts Israel as an immature son (Gal. 3:23), the Church as an adult son and heir (Gal. 3:25–26). At a dramatic moment in the Roman ceremony of adoption, the new heir is clothed with the magnificent *toga virilis*, the garment of manhood.

> For all of you who were baptized into Christ [the baptism of the Holy Spirit] have clothed yourselves with Christ. (Gal. 3:27, NASB)

Christians wear the spiritual equivalent of the *toga virilis* from the moment of salvation, when the baptism of the Spirit occurs. Through the merits of Christ, Church Age believers are adopted as adult sons of God and joint heirs with Christ at the first instant of faith in Him (Rom. 8:16–17; Eph. 1:5). Although a spiritual infant in experience, every Church Age believer is a spiritual adult in position. He is granted the full privileges and responsibilities of an adult son of God because he is in union with the Lord Jesus Christ.

## THE PROTOCOL PLAN OF GOD

Union with Christ opens the door to an extraordinary postsalvation way of life for the royal family. I call this the *protocol plan of God*. Royalty lives by protocol—spiritual royalty no less so than temporal royalty. The refined behavior and high standards of conduct in a vigorous aristocracy are supported by a system of protocol. Each individual is thoroughly familiar with the manner in which various activities are conducted. He knows his place in these activities. Protocol enables everyone to know what to do in a given situation and thus creates an environment of poise and graciousness. Protocol resolves routine questions and frees the individual to devote his energies to substantial issues or to enjoying the event at hand.

The Church Age believer need never wonder what the Christian life requires of him. He need not stumble or feel awkward in any aspect of his relationship with God. The entire royal protocol is available for him to learn and master. He belongs to a spiritual dynasty founded by the Lord Jesus Christ in which the standard of conduct follows the precedent clearly established by the humanity of Christ on earth. In the Church Age, the *protocol* plan of God for the Church supersedes the *ritual* plan of God for Israel.

Protocol is defined as a "rigid long-established code prescribing complete deference to superior rank and strict adherence to due order of precedence and precisely correct procedure."[65] The several phrases of this definition illustrate God's plan for the royal family on earth.

Although new to history at the beginning of the Church Age, the protocol plan is "long-established" in the mind of omniscient God. He has always known the way of life He would unveil for the Church Age. He has known the mystery doctrines from eternity past (Eph. 3:9), and in historical terms these doctrines have been in force now for nearly two thousand years.

The exactness of God's code for spiritual royalty expresses His own perfection: He decreed one way of doing something, and that way is the right way. We cannot define the Christian way of life in any way we please. God "prescribes complete deference" to the ends and the means of *His* plan. The very concept of protocol means that even a right thing becomes wrong when done in a wrong way. And a wrong thing is still wrong though done in a right way. Obviously a wrong thing done in a wrong way is wrong. Only a right thing done in a right way is right. This is "precisely correct procedure."

The *right thing* is the protocol plan of God. The *right way* demanded by protocol is life in the divine dynasphere. Therefore, the most basic concept of the Christian way of life is residence, function, and momentum inside the divine dynasphere. The divine dynasphere is the royal believer's personal, invisible palace.

God is eternally and infinitely perfect. Perfect God can devise only a perfect plan. However, the protocol plan of God, like His post-

---

65. *Webster's Third New International Dictionary*, s.v. "protocol."

salvation plans for other dispensations, is designed for imperfect believers. Because the Christian retains his sin nature throughout his mortal life on earth (1 John 1:8–10), his contribution to the plan of God would only corrupt the plan. The believer cannot execute God's protocol plan through human ability, human dynamics, human personality, human intelligence, human talent, or human works. If the plan of God depended on man's merit for a single instant, the plan would immediately become imperfect. God allows no weak links in the chain. He guards the integrity of His plan. This is grace. Man *enters* God's perfect plan exclusively on the merits of Christ, and the principle of grace remains in force *after* salvation as well. The believer lives the Christian life on divine resources only (Eph. 4:20–24).

Perfect God has provided His perfect truth (Eph. 4:21*b*, 24–25, 29) and His own power (Eph. 4:30*a*) for the execution of His protocol plan. Truth and falsehood do not mix without becoming false. Therefore, divine viewpoint from Bible doctrine must replace human viewpoint. Likewise, divine power and human power are mutually exclusive. Observing divine protocol must take precedence over the expression of human abilities (1 Cor. 2:4–5). Human innovation must remain within bounds of the system God has ordained. The truth and the power of the Holy Spirit, on which the humanity of Christ relied during the great power experiment of the hypostatic union, define the only correct approach to life for every believer during the great power experiment of the Church Age.

Contradictions cannot exist in the protocol plan of God. Either a believer will utilize the available omnipotence of God and execute the protocol plan, or he will use human energy in an attempt to execute an inferior plan of his own. Many people presumptuously call their own plans the plan of God or the will of God, when in fact these schemes may be satanic counterfeits designed to entangle believers in the evils of religion (1 Tim. 4:1).[66] Faithful intake and application of Bible doctrine protect the believer from such contradictions.

---

66. Christianity is not a religion. Christianity is a personal relationship with God established by the work of Christ. Religion is man's futile attempt through his own efforts to achieve a relationship with God. See Thieme, *Christian Integrity*, 146–58, for a presentation of Satan's cosmic system, which includes religion.

The Christian who is ignorant of Church Age doctrine, however, lacks discernment. He is incapable of grace orientation. He cannot be true to his spiritual heritage. Ignorance mixed with negligence cannot avoid the trap of arrogance. He assumes he is doing God's will even as he falls into Satan's cosmic system and becomes a loser in the great power experiment of the Church Age. Losers do not lose their salvation, but in failing to execute the postsalvation protocol plan of God, they lose blessing and impact in time and eternity.

At physical birth man is born ignorant of life. Likewise, at spiritual birth[67] believers are "born again" ignorant of the protocol plan of God. Human opinion or philosophy, despite its occasional brilliance, never determines the Christian way of life (1 Cor. 1:20–31). What matters is what God has revealed in the mystery doctrine of the Church Age. No believer can execute the protocol plan without learning and applying Bible doctrine.

## MYSTERY DOCTRINE

We have noted already that the Greek noun *musterion* originally referred to the secret doctrines of ancient religious organizations. Only those persons initiated into the cult of Dionysus, for example, knew its mysteries. Nothing was disclosed to outsiders. Paul borrowed this well-known pagan term to communicate the divine truths of the royal family of God. In Paul's usage of *musterion*, the initiates are Church Age believers, and the doctrines are those concerned with the Church. God did not disclose Church doctrine to the writers of Old Testament Scripture, but these marvelous truths now are revealed throughout the New Testament epistles (Rom. 16:25–26; Eph. 3:1–9; Col. 1:25–28).

> But we communicate God's wisdom in a mystery, [which communicates] the hidden [assets], which God predestined[68] before the ages [in eternity past, before the dispensations of human history] to our glory [the Church Age

---

67. Spiritual birth is regeneration at the moment of faith in Christ. See Thieme, *The Integrity of God*, 94, 110–14.

68. See page 108.

believer's utilization of divine assets, which glorifies God in the great power experiment of the Church Age]. (1 Cor. 2:7)

With a pure conscience, keep holding the mystery, even doctrine. (1 Tim. 3:9)

Mystery doctrine reveals all the *politeuma* privileges of the Church Age believer, which sets the Church Age apart from other dispensations. The mandate to "keep holding the mystery" identifies the most vital function of the royal family: to continually learn, retain, and apply the doctrines of the Church. Hearing doctrine, meditating on doctrine, living by doctrine is the highest form of worship. The royal family of God has a unique potential to worship God because of the unprecedented extent of divine revelation in the mystery doctrine (Eph. 3:18).

# THE PORTFOLIO OF INVISIBLE ASSETS

## *The Believer's Wealth Taught by Analogy*

We have discussed three *politeuma* privileges. The baptism of the Holy Spirit places the Church Age believer into union with Christ. The protocol plan of God sets forth the royal way of life that God expects of the Christian because of his exalted position in Christ. And mystery doctrine unveils the Church Age with all of its divine assets and mandates which define the Christian's way of life.

These three tremendous benefits of our heavenly citizenship are parts of a larger picture. They belong to a *portfolio of invisible assets* that God the Father designed in eternity past for every Church Age believer. Portfolio is a term for the holdings of an investor, a synonym for his riches. God has lavished the riches of His grace upon us (Eph. 1:6–8, 18; 3:8, 16; Phil. 4:19; Col. 1:27; 2:2). Every Church Age believer is fabulously wealthy.

Blessed *be* the God and Father of our Lord Jesus Christ, who [the Father] has blessed us with every spiritual blessing in the heavenly *places* in Christ. (Eph. 1:3, NASB)

Not only is the Church Age believer a citizen of heaven but that citizenship implies extreme wealth. "Our *politeuma* is in heaven" (Phil. 3:20), and our portfolio is described as including "every spiritual blessing in the heavenly places" (Eph. 1:3). Ephesians 1:3 emphasizes the source of these blessings (God the Father) and the mechanics of receiving them (from Christ). We will explain these mechanics shortly.

The believer's portfolio of invisible assets can be categorized. Ephesians 1:3–6 identifies the primary assets; the secondary and personnel assets will be identified from other passages of Scripture.

1. *Primary assets.*
   a. Escrow Blessings.
   b. Computer Assets.
2. *Secondary assets.*
   a. Volitional Assets.
   b. Production Assets.
   c. Assets for Undeserved Suffering.
3. *Personnel assets.*
   Spiritual Gifts.

I have adopted two analogies to help communicate the Christian's primary assets. I call them his *escrow blessings* and his *computer assets*. In Ephesians 1:3, the phrase "every spiritual blessing in the heavenly places in Christ" describes escrow blessings. In verses 4 through 6, election and predestination constitute the computer assets.

The Church Age believer's exalted destiny and vast riches are "exceeding abundantly beyond all that we ask or think" (Eph. 3:20). The Bible reveals them in many glimpses and increments; they must be explained in numerous ways and from various points of view. Therefore, analogy plays an important role in teaching the Christian way of life. Already we have approached the subject from the standpoint of citizenship, Roman adoption, parts of the body, aristocratic protocol, the secret doctrines of an exclusive religion, and an investment portfolio. Now add the perspectives of an escrow contract and a computer.

The analogies I devise are teaching aids and are not intended to perfectly mesh with one another. Each serves to communicate a specific aspect of the truth. The truth itself is what perfectly meshes.

## *Escrow Blessings*

### INHERITANCE RESERVED IN HEAVEN

Three parties are identified in Ephesians 1:3. The relationship between God the Father, Jesus Christ, and the Church Age believer in this passage suggests the functions of a grantor, a depositary, and a grantee in an escrow contract. What is an escrow contract? It is a binding agreement in which one party gives another party something valuable. Instead of giving it directly, however, the grantor places the item in the custody of a third party, called the depositary or the escrow officer. The escrow officer keeps the item secure and distributes it to the grantee only after certain conditions are met, which have been set forth in the escrow agreement.

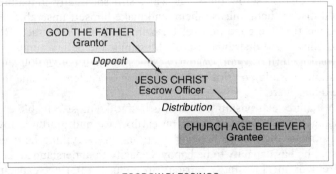

GOD THE FATHER
Grantor

*Deposit*

JESUS CHRIST
Escrow Officer

*Distribution*

CHURCH AGE BELIEVER
Grantee

ESCROW BLESSINGS

The very definition of escrow means there are conditions to be fulfilled by the grantee before the item will be conveyed to him. An escrow agreement gives us a clear picture of our situation before God and our purpose in life.

In eternity past God the Father prepared special blessings for each Church Age believer. He deposited those blessings with Christ "before the foundation of the world" (Eph. 1:4). Just as an escrow contract is irrevocable from the date of the contract, so also the believer's blessings belong to him irrevocably from eternity past. God has given every Church Age believer a private account in heaven, which He cannot cancel or close. God cannot take back His blessings. This account is filled with exceptional blessings—some for time, some for eternity. God designed escrow blessings exclusively for each individual believer, an "inheritance which is imperishable and undefiled and will not fade away, reserved in heaven for [him]" (1 Pet. 1:4).

Escrow blessings far exceed everyday logistical blessings like food, shelter, clothing, protection, transportation, and a source of Bible teaching.[69] God supplies logistical grace constantly and unconditionally to every believer—positive or negative, winner or loser (Matt. 6:25–34; Phil. 4:19; cf., 4:2–3). Escrow blessings, however, are reserved for spiritual maturity.

So extraordinary are these "greater grace" blessings (James 4:6) that every recipient must possess a mature capacity to appreciate them and benefit from them. Without sufficient capacity of soul, a believer would not know what to do with these divine bounties. If he received delivery of his escrow blessings while still spiritually immature, he would distort them, misuse them, and make himself miserable. Here, then, we find the condition set forth in the escrow contract: Before Jesus Christ will distribute escrow blessings, the believer must attain spiritual maturity. Again, maturity comes through perception and application of Bible doctrine as part of living consistently inside the divine dynasphere.

A mature relationship with God is by far the most valuable escrow blessing for the Christian's life on earth. Awe and gratitude toward God animate the mature believer's attitude in everything he does. In his soul he has capacity to be happy, capacity to understand and benefit from divine blessings, capacity to endure suffering, capacity to maintain the initiative in his own life. He has a personal sense of destiny. Worship becomes a profound responsiveness in a soul inculcated with truth and filled with the Spirit (John 7:38). Personal love for God becomes occupation with the Person of Christ (Gal. 2:20; Phil. 1:21). But "every spiritual blessing" involves more than even these marvelous, intangible benefits. "Spiritual" in Ephesians 1:3 points to God as the source of escrow blessings, which also include many tangible and material blessings, tailor-made for the individual.

---

69. Thieme, *The Integrity of God*, 30, 90–91.

## BLESSINGS FOR TIME AND ETERNITY

Every believer has escrow blessings for time and escrow blessings for eternity. Examples of these blessings are presented in *The Integrity of God*.[70] As the escrow officer Jesus Christ will begin to distribute *escrow blessings for time* when the believer reaches spiritual maturity. Our Lord will award *escrow blessings for eternity* at the judgment seat of Christ, which will occur immediately after the Rapture of the Church (1 Cor. 4:5; 2 Cor. 5:10).

Believers who fail to reach spiritual maturity and do not receive their escrow blessings for time, also will not receive their escrow blessings for eternity (1 Cor. 3:12–15). The criterion is human volition—each believer's consistent positive or negative response to God's plan for the Christian life. After salvation, what? The great question has eternal repercussions. In the escrow contract, the precondition for receiving escrow blessings for eternity is that the believer must have received escrow blessings in time.

> Now if anyone really competes in the athletic games [an analogy to the Christian way of life], he does not receive a winner's wreath [escrow blessings for eternity] unless he trains according to the rules [adheres to the protocol plan of God]. (2 Tim. 2:5)

> I have fought that honorable fight [advanced through the stages of spiritual growth], I have finished the course [attained maturity], I have guarded the doctrine [as first priority in the soul]. In the future a wreath of righteousness [escrow blessings for eternity] is reserved for me [on deposit since eternity past], which the Lord, the righteous judge, will award me on that day [at the judgment seat of Christ] and not only to me but to all those who love His appearing [mature believers, whose thorough understanding of doctrine enables them to be occupied with Christ]. (2 Tim. 4:7–8)

> Blessed [happy] is the man who perseveres under testing [successfully passes the tests that accelerate spiritual

---

70. Ibid., 114–50.

growth];[71] he will receive the wreath of life [escrow blessings for eternity] which God has promised to those constantly loving Him [mature believers]. (James 1:12)

These passages describe desire for truth, love for God, strength of character, remarkable stability, perseverance, motivation, momentum, and happiness. Such qualities of the inner person are escrow blessings for time. They are escrow blessings supported by the basic capacities of soul developed on the way to maturity. Invariably these traits—these escrow blessings for time—belong to the believers whom Scripture identifies as recipients of eternal rewards or "crowns"—their escrow blessings for eternity (1 Cor. 9:24–27; Phil. 4:1; 1 Thess. 2:19–20; 1 Pet. 5:1–4; Rev. 2:10). Distribution of both categories of escrow blessings—for time and for eternity—depends on the believer's execution of the protocol plan of God in time. The precondition for receiving escrow blessings dramatizes God's objective for the Church Age believer on earth: Learn Bible doctrine, gain spiritual momentum, grow up, attain maturity! In other words, come to love and glorify Christ.

## UNDISTRIBUTED BLESSINGS AND THE GLORY OF GOD

At this moment each believer has an escrow account in heaven with his name on it. But not every believer takes distribution of those blessings. Ignorance of Bible doctrine means ignorance of divine assets, which guarantees failure to use those assets. Failure to consistently utilize divine assets constitutes failure to execute the protocol plan of God, which means the believer cannot reach spiritual maturity. If there is no maturity, then there is no capacity for blessings; therefore, no escrow blessings for time, and no escrow blessings for eternity (1 Cor. 3:11–15). This does not affect his salvation, but his neglect or rejection of Bible doctrine makes him a spiritual loser.

There is no excuse for failure to execute the protocol plan of God. God faithfully supplies logistical grace to winner and loser alike, providing more than ample opportunity for the loser to recover his momentum and renew his advance. Equal privilege and equal opportunity are facts of the Christian way of life, and the escrow blessings them-

---

71. For a description of momentum testing, see Thieme, *Christian Suffering*, 128–47.

selves are irrevocable and imperishable realities. If a believer is a spiritual loser, he is so by his own volition. A loser stops being a loser when he starts using rebound and begins to learn, or relearn, Bible doctrine. Recovery of spiritual momentum is not easy, but it will never be easier than at present. Recovery can begin in any spiritual condition in which the loser finds himself. There is no reason to wait. There is nothing to wait for and much to lose.

If the loser does not recover, his personal inheritance of escrow blessings will remain undistributed, unreceived, on deposit in heaven forever. At the resurrection of the Church, the loser will receive his resurrection body and will enjoy perfect happiness in heaven, but he will not receive his escrow blessings for eternity (1 Cor. 3:15). They will remain on deposit forever as a monument to lost opportunity and as undeniable evidence of God's grace in spite of man's negative volition (Eph. 1:3; 3:10; 1 Pet. 1:3–4).

God was glorified by irrevocably giving escrow blessings to each believer "before the foundation of the world" (Eph. 1:4; Col. 3:24; 1 Pet. 1:4). God is glorified to the maximum by the distribution of these escrow blessings to the spiritual winner in time and eternity. Describing God at the beginning of Ephesians 1:3, the Greek adjective εὐλογητός (*eulogetos*) is translated "blessed," but this word actually means "worthy of praise and glorification." In the same verse the verb is εὐλογέω (*eulogeo*), "to bless." Furthermore, the cognate noun εὐλογία (*eulogia*) is used for the believer's "blessings." Blessed, bless, blessings: This dramatic use of Greek cognate words indicates an essential interconnection. These blessings are the means of God's glorification. He is glorified by blessing us. Principle: The first thing God did for us—placing special blessings in escrow—established the means of glorifying Him. God's desire that we receive our escrow blessings could not be expressed more emphatically.

What do we conclude? Obviously, asceticism is *not* the Christian way of life (Col. 2:20–23). But neither is aimless, undisciplined lawlessness (2 Tim. 2:5). The Church Age believer has a destiny. He glorifies God by utilizing divine assets so that he grows spiritually and acquires capacity to enjoy his escrow blessings.

God created escrow blessings for every believer of every dispensation, but the greater extent of the Church Age believer's portfolio makes even his escrow blessings unique. We come now to an exceedingly valuable item in the royal believer's portfolio that sets his blessings apart from those of all other dispensations.

## Computer Assets

*A MODERN ANALOGY*

Again, the Christian's portfolio of invisible assets includes two categories of primary assets. We have described escrow blessings; we now turn our attention to *computer assets*. I use this term to describe the Church Age believer's election and predestination.

> Just as He [God the Father] *chose* us in Him [in union with Christ] before the foundation of the world, that we should be holy and blameless before Him [God's purpose in election includes positional and experiential sanctification on earth and ultimate sanctification in heaven]. In love He *predestined* us to adoption as sons through Jesus Christ to Himself [as in the Roman custom of adoption], according to the kind intention of His will, to the praise of the glory of His grace, which He freely bestowed on us in the Beloved [in union with Christ]. (Eph. 1:4–6, NASB, italics added)

What are "election" and "predestination"? How do they affect us? In brief, God has established a plan and has supplied us with all assets needed to execute that plan.

Computers are a familiar part of daily life. A simple analogy to a computer might help to make this passage clear. The complex functions of a computer occur in tiny electrical circuits built into a microchip of silicon no larger than the head of a pin.

Different microchips perform specialized functions in the computer. Two common types of these powerful chips illustrate how liberally sovereign God has blessed Church Age believers without nullifying their volition. In fact, this computer analogy helps explain how God Himself establishes human free will.[72]

---

72. I also use a computer analogy to illustrate the doctrine of divine decrees (see Thieme, *The Integrity of God*, Appendix B). The "computer assets" in the believer's portfolio, however, are a different analogy. They describe the individual Church Age believer rather than

A computer contains a certain number of microchips. Some chips are completely programmed at the factory, others are designed at the factory to be programmed by the user—according to what he wants his computer to be able to do. Both the ROM chips (Read-Only Memory, programmed at the factory) and the PROM chips (Programmable Read-Only Memory, built at the factory to be programmed by the user himself) cannot be altered once they are programmed. And both are necessary for the effective function of the computer.

Like the computer, the believer's life involves both divine sovereignty (comparable to the ROM chips programmed in advance at the factory) and human volition (comparable to the PROM chips that are programmed by the user's own decisions). Just as a particular computer would not operate without both types of programmed microchips, so also human thought and action cannot occur without the function of both divine sovereignty and human volition.

Indeed, God is the One who makes our volition free. He gave man free will, just as the factory designs the computer's PROM chips specifically to let the user determine how the computer will function. The user's programming of his own PROM chip works only because of the designer's plan: The factory design of the PROM chip takes the user's programming and makes it effective. In a similar way, God sovereignly makes man's free choices real, certain, and unalterable once they are made.

According to the analogy, each person is like a computer. His ROM chip (programmed entirely by the sovereignty of God) is programmed with his computer assets. He has no choice in this matter. Long before human history began, God unilaterally chose to give the Church Age believer certain characteristics. He chose to make the Christian spiritual royalty—as it were, to make him the most powerful computer ever created. This means that the computer assets of election and predestination include tremendous benefits, which God gave in eternity past. We are now studying these benefits as the unique characteristics of the Church Age.

The ROM chip contains God's plan and gives every Church Age believer the status and assets required to carry out this demanding

---

the whole of God's decree in eternity past. The computer that contains everything should not be confused with the computer that illustrates one believer's life.

protocol. The PROM chip (programmed the way human volition chooses) gives us the freedom to use those powerful assets if we so desire.
The PROM chip makes us spiritual winners or losers, according to our
decisions to use divine assets and fulfill God's plan—or to ignore our
spiritual destiny in Christ.

## DIVINE SOVEREIGNTY AND CHRISTIAN FREEDOM

The computer analogy helps us understand what the sovereignty
and omniscience of God accomplished in eternity past on behalf of the
Church Age believer. The blessings mentioned in Ephesians 1:5–6 are
some of the unique characteristics of the Church Age that we have already discussed. In eternity past God determined that *sanctification*
and *adoption* would be given to the royal family through union with
Christ. As also noted, we have no choice in this matter: At the moment
of faith in Christ, these blessings are ours and we are new creatures in
Christ, a new spiritual species. The mechanics by which God established these and other characteristics of the Church Age believer involved election and predestination.

Election expresses the sovereign right of God over His creation.[73]
Election can be described in terms of individuals and in terms of
groups. God elected for salvation every human being who would ever
believe in Jesus Christ. Election is not the cause of salvation. Instead,
God sovereignly chose to accomplish all the work for man's salvation
and to institute nonmeritorious faith in Jesus Christ as the sole remaining criterion for obtaining salvation. Because divine omniscience is
not limited by time, God knew in eternity past who would believe in
Christ and in eternity past chose each *believer* to be the recipient of
eternal salvation. In other words, He chose to make salvation a reality
in the soul of anyone who actually would believe in Christ. Therefore,
every believer of every dispensation can be described as elect in regard to salvation.

Election also is a biblical term that carries additional significance
for particular historical groups of believers. Here is yet another category of doctrine that reflects dispensational distinctions. Election to
salvation gives every believer the necessities for living with God for-

---

73. A more detailed study of election and predestination is presented in audio recordings
available without charge as noted on page *iv*.

ever—including eternal life and divine righteousness. But added to these identical provisions, further blessings are bestowed upon specified groups of believers at the moment of salvation. These are designed to fulfill God's purpose beyond salvation.

The position and assets bestowed at the moment of salvation upon members of the royal family are more extensive than the blessings given to believers of other dispensations.[74] God elected Church Age believers for a unique, corporate purpose beyond salvation. The special destiny of the royal family in both time and eternity is to glorify God to the maximum in union with Jesus Christ.

The election of the Church is one of several corporate divine elections, three of which are pertinent to our study.[75]

1. *The election of Israel* (Deut. 4:37; 7:6; Isa. 45:4; Matt. 24:22, 24, 31; Rom. 11:5–7).
2. *The election of Christ* (Isa. 42:1; Eph. 4:1; 1 Pet. 2:6).
3. *The election of the Church* (Eph. 4:1; 1 Thess. 1:4; 2 Thess. 2:13; 2 Pet. 1:3).

A thread of continuity runs through these three expressions of divine sovereignty, but the differences also are real and significant. These three unique elections express God's purpose in three distinct dispensations: 1) the election of Israel—God called out the Jews as a new racial species to bless all the nations of the earth, 2) the election of Christ—God called out Christ as the Savior to purchase the salvation of the entire human race and to be exalted above all creation, and 3) the election of the Church—God called out a royal family as a new spiritual species to glorify the newly-won royalty of Jesus Christ forever.

As part of our *politeuma* privileges, therefore, election is the sovereign expression in eternity past of God's will for the Church Age believer. Under election, God the Father willed His highest and best for every Church Age believer, having previously deposited His highest and best for us with Christ. In short, God's will for our lives is that we receive what belongs to the glorified Christ.

---

74. The Church Age believer receives at least forty things from God at the instant of salvation. See Thieme, *The Plan of God* (2003); *Rebound Revisited* (1995).

75. Other corporate elections include the Levites and the family of Aaron (Num. 17—18) and the 144,000 Jewish evangelists of the Tribulation (Rev. 7:4–8).

> *I pray that* the eyes of your heart may be enlightened,
> so that you may know what is the hope of His calling,
> what are the riches of the glory of His inheritance in
> the saints, and what is the surpassing greatness of His
> power [the divine dynasphere] toward us who believe.
> *These are* in accordance with the working of the
> strength of His might which He brought about in
> Christ, when He raised Him from the dead, and seated
> Him at His right hand in the heavenly *places* [invest-
> ing Christ with 'battlefield' royalty for His victory at
> the cross], far above all rule and authority and power
> and dominion, and every name that is named, not only
> in this age, but also in the one to come [the permanent
> resolution of the angelic conflict]. And He put all
> things in subjection under His feet, and gave Him as
> head over all things to the church, which is His body,
> the fulness of Him who fills all in all. (Eph. 1:18–23,
> NASB)

This is the purpose for which God called us out and set us apart: to
exalt the royalty of Christ to the maximum. Our election creates the
special privileges and opportunities necessary for us to receive the
blessings of spiritual royalty which glorify Christ.

Election and predestination are two sides of the same coin. God
chose us to glorify Christ to the maximum and chose to accomplish
this purpose according to a definite plan. The election of the Church is
the *expression* of the sovereign will of God for every believer of the
Church Age; predestination is the *provision* of His sovereign will. In
time this divine provision is classified as the protocol plan of God, but
when discussed in the context of eternity past, this provision is called
predestination.

Long before human history began, God sovereignly established a
supernatural way of life for the Church Age believer and provided the
supernatural means of execution. Predestination implies that the only
way to fulfill the plan of God for our lives is to properly utilize the assets He has given us. We are free to make good use of the computer or
to ignore its great potential, but the computer works in a particular
manner. We must learn how to use it and then must use it properly. A
principle summarizes the Church Age believer's computer assets: The

Christian is designed to live the Christian way of life. From the believer's functional perspective this means that a right thing must be done in a right way.

## Enlarging the Portfolio with Secondary Assets

The believer's use of his computer assets actually enlarges his portfolio. In eternity past God the Father established the Church Age believer's primary assets (escrow blessings and computer assets). Then God added *secondary assets* to the portfolio corresponding to the positive response of the believer in time.

How does this work? In eternity past omniscient God looked down the corridors of time, as it were, and saw how each believer would use his volition: positive or negative, for or against the protocol plan of God. Without interfering with human free will (in fact, *because* of free will), God included secondary assets in the positive believer's portfolio based on his use of his primary assets.

Secondary assets are not second in importance or quality. They simply come after primary assets in the sequence in which man understands them, and they involve human volition. But they are blessings from God just as certainly as the primary assets.

In terms of our analogy that compares a believer with a computer, primary assets are on ROM chips, and secondary assets are on PROM chips. Primary assets originate from the sovereignty of God and represent His design for the believer's life. Secondary assets also originate from the sovereignty of God, but rather than representing God's will alone they reflect the individual believer's own consistent positive response to the grace of God. The sovereignty of God and the free will of the believer coexist in the dynamics of the Christian way of life. The secondary assets, which we are about to study, exist because God saw to it in eternity past that the powerful computer of the Church Age believer would work. He programmed it exactly as decided by both His divine sovereignty and the believer's free will.

Only the advancing believer receives secondary assets, which are God's response to his positive volition. For the indifferent or recalcitrant believer, the counterpart to secondary assets is divine discipline, which is God's response to his negative volition.

By giving us freedom of choice, God has also given us the effects and consequences of our decisions. If our decisions had no effect, we would not be free. But God did indeed decree that the results of our decisions actually would take place. He made our volition efficacious. He made us responsible for our own lives. This means that a positive response to the plan of God has a real effect. He made the consistently positive believer a winner. A negative response also has a real effect, but God will allow a believer to be a loser only to a certain degree, for he cannot lose his salvation. This is grace, the efficacy of Christ's work on the cross.

Two important lessons are found in the very existence of secondary assets. First, no matter how hopeless a believer's situation may seem, making good decisions is never an exercise in futility. Learning and relying upon Bible doctrine and consistently residing in the divine dynasphere *do* make a difference, a difference that God established in eternity past in the form of secondary assets.

There is yet another lesson. By giving the mandates of the protocol plan of God—and thus directing our free will along the lines of His sovereign purpose—God makes it possible for our lives to accomplish His will. Our obedience to His plan has the real effect of achieving His objective. God in His infinite superiority does not simply go about His affairs without us. The effects and consequences of our decisions can be magnificent, eternally rewardable demonstrations of His glory. This gives our lives genuine meaning, purpose, and definition.

God knows all things at once. Omniscient and eternal, He knows the end from the beginning, the causes and results as a single whole. He knows about time and the progression of events, but time does not restrict His knowledge. He comprehends all things as one complete and total picture. The logic of all things is in Him; He needs no time in which to deliberate. Before He created time, God established the future reality of both primary and secondary assets in one all-comprehensive decree.[76]

Limited human faculties require believers to think of primary and secondary assets in increments, as a succession of cause and effect. For us something becomes real when we experience it or do it, but for

---

76. Thieme, *The Integrity of God*, Appendix B.

God all things became certain in eternity past when He decreed them to be reality. Thus infinite God knew each of us and worked on our behalf long before we existed. This means we belong to a plan that extends far beyond the circumstances of the moment. Not only is God near—an ever-present help in time of need—but He has woven His help into the very fabric of our lives as we unfold our lives in time.

God provided all categories of assets in eternity past, but they are delivered at various points in time. The Christian receives his computer assets at salvation. He takes delivery of escrow blessings as he moves into spiritual maturity. Between these two points he begins to receive secondary assets as he grows spiritually. Three kinds of secondary assets should be noted.

1. *Volitional assets.*
2. *Production assets.*
3. *Assets for undeserved suffering.*

How are secondary assets different from other divine blessings? One outstanding difference is that secondary assets are tangible. Many advantages in the Christian way of life are intangible. Some lie beyond human experience (like union with Christ or the filling of the Spirit). Some are abstract (like doctrinal concepts). Others are reserved for the future (like dying grace, perhaps, or escrow blessings for eternity). All these invisible blessings are nonetheless real.

The believer's secondary assets are also real, but these blessings related to volition, production, and suffering are advantages that the advancing believer begins to experience in his everyday life. These are the assets that James has in mind when he encourages believers to grow up—to be "doers of the Word and not merely hearers who delude themselves" (James 1:22). In other words, intangible advantages mixed with positive volition produce tangible results.

## Volitional Assets

### GOOD DECISIONS FROM A POSITION OF STRENGTH

Positive volition is an active desire to know God. It is love for truth, which expresses itself in persistently learning the Word of God and consistently living by its precepts. All secondary assets result from the believer's positive volition toward Bible doctrine, and one of these secondary assets is the strengthening of positive volition itself. Knowledge builds on knowledge. The more Bible doctrine a believer knows, the greater his frame of reference for comprehending additional doctrine. Thus, good decisions to learn the Word of God create options for further good decisions to keep learning. As the believer's capacity for doctrine expands, his love for Bible doctrine increases because truth and wisdom are intrinsically worthy of love (Prov. 8:30–31).

This sharpened receptivity to truth rests upon an invisible foundation. The growing believer's keener discernment and stronger desire for doctrine may seem to be only a natural result of broadening his doctrinal frame of reference. However, the Christian should appreciate the invisible work of God and recognize that even the maturing of his own positive volition is from God. Spiritual growth itself is a gift of grace.

Advancement to spiritual maturity requires a consistent pattern of good decisions made from a position of strength. Good decisions are those that obey the mandates of divine protocol—for example, decisions to listen to Bible teaching or to utilize divine problem-solving devices. This is the *tangible*, or conscious, aspect of the believer's positive volition. The position of strength is the divine dynasphere, in which the Holy Spirit makes Bible doctrine understandable and uses the believer's store of doctrine to fuel his spiritual momentum. The Holy Spirit supplies the *intangible*, unfelt effectiveness of the believer's positive volition. This invisible dimension, which the Christian does not experience, is disclosed only in the content of doctrine. Knowledge of the Spirit's unseen role gives the Christian a sense of gratitude for increases in his desire for truth, comprehension of doctrine, and personal love for God, all of which he does experience.

## THE VISIBLE AND THE INVISIBLE

This duality stands out dramatically in salvation and continues *after* salvation in God's grace policy for dealing with the royal family (1 Cor. 2:4–5; cf., 2:10). Man gains salvation through faith in Christ. However, before he believes in Christ for salvation, he is spiritually dead (Eph. 2:1). He is totally depraved, totally separated from God, and totally helpless to establish a relationship with God. Faith originating from a spiritually dead person has no power in itself to produce so great a result as salvation. The apparent cause (nonmeritorious faith) and the actual effect (eternal salvation) are completely out of

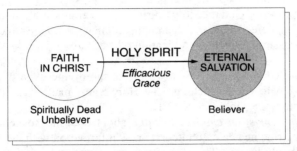

SALVATION THROUGH FAITH IN CHRIST

proportion with one another. Obviously, an invisible factor is at work. God Himself—not a spiritually dead man's momentary act of faith—is the real cause of salvation.

The entire Trinity was involved in Christ's death and resurrection,[77] and God the Holy Spirit specifically is the agent of salvation. He reveals the Gospel (Gen. 6:3) and makes man's faith in Christ effectual (Eph. 1:13) so that the believer's "faith should not rest on the wisdom of men, but on the power of God" (1 Cor. 2:5). Thus the believer is saved "by grace . . . through faith" (Eph. 2:8–9). His faith is made effective by the power of God the Holy Spirit.[78]

After salvation, the believer is no longer spiritually dead, depraved, or separated from God (Eph. 2:4–5). The Church Age believer possesses fabulous advantages, but his positive volition still lacks the power in itself to advance him spiritually (Gal. 3:3; Eph. 4:20, 23, 30). Spiritual growth is a marvelous *divine* achievement. Simply desiring to grow does not produce growth, nor does slavish adherence to some religious formula—including rigid, unthinking, legalistic attendance to hear Bible teaching. Growth comes not by hoping or striving but as a result of learning, thinking, and solving problems

---

77. Thieme, *Christian Suffering*, 130–32.
78. Thieme, *The Integrity of God*, 93–94.

with Bible doctrine, which is the power of God (Rom. 1:16; Heb. 4:12). But even the keenest human intellect cannot penetrate the mystery doctrine (1 Cor. 2:6–9). How, then, can we grow? Once again the grace of God meets the helplessness of man. He places us in an invisible position of strength.

The power of God the Holy Spirit operates after salvation in the divine dynasphere. The Spirit's communication ministry aids in comprehension, assimilation, and application of the truth.

1. *The Christian chooses to reside* in the divine dynasphere and listen to Bible teaching. The Holy Spirit makes true doctrine comprehensible (1 Cor. 2:12).
2. *The Christian chooses to think* about doctrine, to believe the doctrine he hears, to integrate new information with the truth he already knows. The Holy Spirit converts academic knowledge of doctrine into genuine understanding (1 Cor. 2:13).
3. *The Christian chooses to apply* doctrine in the circumstances of his life. The Holy Spirit aids in the recall of the truth so that the believer "walks by means of the Spirit" (Gal. 5:16).

In every stage of learning, meditating upon, and using doctrine, the believer provides the nonmeritorious positive volition, but God the Holy Spirit provides the unseen power—the spiritual IQ—for comprehending, assimilating, and applying Bible doctrine.

## CHANGES IN POSITIVE VOLITION

The Holy Spirit's communication ministry is powerful but deliberately invisible. The teaching is spotlighted, not the Teacher. He operates in silent support of the normal, human learning process (Rom. 12:2; 2 Tim. 2:15). As far as conscious experience is concerned, the believer listens to Bible teaching, thinks about it, mulls it over, accepts what he believes is true, and lives by the truth. He recognizes the importance the Bible gives to being filled with the Spirit (Gal. 5:16–26; Eph. 4:30; 5:18; 1 Thess. 5:19), so he obeys this mandate by faith. The Holy Spirit's indispensable aid operates below the surface. The Spirit glorifies Christ rather than Himself (John 16:13–14). He illuminates the "mind [thinking] of Christ" (1 Cor. 2:10–16). The Church Age believer "knows" the Spirit but "beholds" Christ, in contrast to the world which neither beholds nor knows the Holy Spirit (John 14:16–19).

Intellectually aware that this invisible power animates the Christian way of life, the believer can all the more appreciate the facets of positive volition which *are* perceptible. As he grows, his positive volition itself changes. Beyond simply opting to hear, accept, or apply Bible doctrine, positive volition becomes an expression of his own spiritual autonomy. Firmly grounded in truth, his doctrinal thinking becomes his outlook on life. He acquires a scale of values in which his relationship with God has first priority. Confidence in God enables him to squarely and honestly face his own questions, as an essential part of being receptive to truth. Doctrine fills all the compartments of his soul, including his subconscious, so that he develops the instincts of grace, of gratitude, of true worship. "Because of practice" in learning and applying doctrine, he has his "senses trained to discern good and evil" (Heb. 5:14). He stretches forward, extending his stride like a runner with the goal in sight (Phil. 3:14). He loves and desires truth. In other words, positive volition becomes an asset in itself, a secondary asset in the believer's now-enlarged portfolio, an asset that becomes the driving force in his life.

The increasing desire to know and worship God propels the potential winner toward his spiritual destiny. He is still free; he still has his sin nature; he can still turn aside into error or indifference. But after his positive volition strengthens into a functioning secondary asset, his frame of reference and his conscience operate in favor of truth. He has forward momentum. Negative volition would go against his own grain.

## VOLITION REMAINS FREE

Positive volition is never automatic, however. Any believer can become "dull of hearing" (Heb. 5:11). Emphasizing the Christian's responsibility to be diligent, Hebrews 6:1–6 warns against departing from Bible doctrine after having built a foundation of elementary knowledge. This passage is especially pertinent because here advancing believers lose their own momentum by ignoring dispensational distinctions. Their initial, accurate frame of reference, or "foundation," is depicted in this context as a list of basic doctrines that begins with "repentance from dead works" and continues through the doctrine of "eternal judgment" (Heb. 6:1*b*–2).

At some point the Christians to whom this epistle was addressed began to neglect the basics they had learned. They found themselves attracted to the traditional Jewish forms of worship that anticipated Christ. Old Testament ritual was legitimate in previous dispensations but was made obsolete by the cross. It has no place in Church Age worship. These Christians "again cruci[ied] to themselves the Son of God" by offering animal sacrifices. Their participation in these ceremonies obscured Church Age doctrine and halted their spiritual growth. As long as they practiced this outmoded ritual, subscribing to the false doctrines involved, it was "impossible to renew them again to repentance" (Heb. 6:6).

This does not mean they could never recover. "Repentance" is the first word from the list of basic doctrines in verse 1. Here, in ancient writing style that conserved valuable space, this initial word represents the entire list. It is impossible to return to basic doctrine and regain spiritual momentum while trusting in dead religious works. Continuing in the wrong direction hardens negative volition,[79] just as consistency in the right direction strengthens positive volition.

## THE ROLE OF ENCOURAGEMENT

Yet another factor plays a discernible role in transforming the believer's positive volition. This factor is encouragement (Phil. 2:1). The invisible resources that God provides for the Church Age believer surpass the imagination. As the Christian establishes a trend of making right decisions, these unseen, primary assets produce their powerful results. He grows up spiritually. Pressures only accelerate his advance. He achieves spiritual self-esteem, spiritual autonomy, and spiritual maturity.[80] The results of executing the protocol plan of God encourage him. His confidence in God continues to grow. This confidence from his own cumulative experience of God's grace strengthens his determination—his positive volition—to keep on fulfilling God's purpose (Phil. 3:12–14).

---

79. Thieme, *Satan and Demonism*, 21–22; *Reversionism* (2000), 18, 29–32.

80. Spiritual self-esteem, spiritual autonomy, and spiritual maturity represent successive stages of spiritual adulthood. See Thieme, *Christian Suffering*.

## Production Assets

The next category of secondary assets concerns Christian service. As a result of spiritual progress, the believer is motivated to do something for the Lord. This desire begins in spiritual childhood and takes definite shape as the believer grows. Genuine Christian service is a privilege, an asset acquired as a result of faithfully adhering to the protocol plan of God. Service is not the first priority for the new believer; doctrine is. And not everything touted as 'Christian service' actually *is* effective Christian service. Discernment in this matter comes from doctrine. Furthermore, even legitimate fields of service can be neutralized by false motivation or the intrusion of human dynamics.

The plan of God operates on divine power, not human power. The believer is completely helpless to make his earthly endeavors count for God. Therefore, God has made His own strength available to each Church Age believer. This power is accessible through the believer's use of his primary assets, which include logistical grace and the divine dynasphere. In eternity past omniscient God knew which believers would utilize their primary assets. He therefore provided effective Christian service in their portfolios as a secondary asset (Eph. 2:10; Phil. 2:13–16; Titus 2:14). True production comes from spiritual growth. Unfortunately, many Christians confuse cause and effect, means and result, vainly attempting to grow up spiritually through the works they perform.

> For we are His creation [the new spiritual species created by the baptism of the Spirit] having been created in Christ Jesus [union with Christ] for good achievements [ἀγαθός, *agathos*, good of intrinsic value] which God [the Father] has prepared in advance [before creation He designed His protocol plan] that we should walk by means of them. (Eph. 2:10)

This passage mentions 1) union with Christ, 2) intrinsically good achievements, and 3) walking (living) by means of those good achievements. As previously noted, union with Christ enables the Church Age believer to utilize God's power in the divine dynasphere. The power of God executes the plan of God so that He Himself is responsible for the spiritual "achievements" in the Christian's life. In eternity past God "prepared in advance" His protocol plan and the divine dynasphere as the means of executing the plan. The believer makes good decisions, but God gets all the credit for the supernatural results.

The believer's consistent positive volition in obeying the mandates of the divine dynasphere becomes spiritual momentum. Momentum includes understanding and using invisible assets, gaining a grace perspective, attaining successive stages of spiritual adulthood. All of these are "intrinsically good achievements," first, because God ordained them as integral parts of His protocol plan for the individual believer and, second, because divine power achieves them.

Christian service is one expression of this spiritual momentum. Christian service itself cannot be called "intrinsically good" because believers can perform acts of Christian service from true or false motives. Service can come from genuine love for God or through legalism or coercion. It can even come from arrogance and self-promotion. This passage emphasizes that true service does not occur in a vacuum. It is not evaluated solely as overt, visible activity but is part of "walking," or living the Christian way of life. The believer lives the Christian life in or, more precisely, "by means of" the stages of spiritual growth that God's power achieves.

Gaining spiritual momentum, which becomes a steady, vigorous Christian walk, implies a sequence that will not work in reverse order. A believer who attempts to advance himself spiritually through the works he performs is wasting his time and squandering his life. He is ignorant of God's protocol, and ignorance breeds arrogance. His motivation is misdirected. He may sincerely want divine approbation, but Jesus is the only human being who ever deserves God's complete approval. Man's only entrée to God is through Christ, according to the protocol God has set forth.

The arrogant Christian's power is merely human and, therefore, cannot produce growth. Spiritual progress does not occur. He runs in vain and toils in vain (Phil. 2:16). He may impress himself and other Christians with his production, but at the judgment seat of Christ this believer's 'Christian service' will be condemned and destroyed as "dead works" (Heb. 6:1; 9:14; cf., 1 Cor. 3:11–15).[81] Jesus Christ as

---

81. Thieme, *Levitical Offerings*, 46–47; *The Integrity of God*, 40, 98; *Christian Integrity*, 154.

the escrow officer will eternally reward only believers whose service reflects spiritual growth, which *is* an intrinsically good achievement. Genuine Christian service is a result of growth and a chance to apply Bible doctrine already assimilated.

Christian production covers a wide range of activities. A partial list shows that different opportunities for legitimate service can appeal to different believers as they advance. Not all Christian service is alike.

1. *Witnessing to unbelievers,* a responsibility of every believer in the course of performing all other categories of Christian service.[82]
2. *Work in the local church,* involving many kinds of service.
3. *Work in Christian service organizations.*
4. *Foreign missionary service.*
5. *Work ordained by the laws of divine establishment,* such as military or government service.
6. *Service to the needy of the community.*
7. *Specialized functions,* such as working with youth or the handicapped or volunteering in a hospital.
8. *The function of one's spiritual gift,* which will be mentioned separately under the Church Age believer's personnel assets.

## Assets for Undeserved Suffering

The final category of secondary assets in the believer's portfolio is suffering for blessing.[83] This asset, like certain aspects of positive volition and service, is an example of continuity in the midst of change. In *every* dispensation God uses suffering as a means of blessing the spiritually adult believer. In His marvelous grace God designed pressures for each stage of a believer's advance in spiritual adulthood. The objective is accelerated spiritual growth.

Christianity is *not* a religion of suffering, regardless of ascetic distortions that have cropped up throughout Church history. Suffering is part of life. We are mortals living in the devil's world among other mortals, all possessing a sin nature. God first of all enables the

---

82. Thieme, *Witnessing.*
83. Thieme, *Christian Suffering,* 62–67.

believer to eliminate self-induced misery from his own life, then He carries out the greatest coup of all. God has incorporated human suffering into His plan. Hence, suffering poses no threat to the plan of God. He uses suffering to advance the believer spiritually. As the believer learns to use the assets God has given him, suffering loses much of its dread.

God uses the right kind and degree of suffering to stretch the believer beyond his human resources, compelling him to rely utterly upon the grace of God. This undeserved suffering is designed to teach the all-sufficiency of God. The believer might fail a test and collapse under pressure, but never is the pressure greater than he can bear if he uses the doctrinal resources in his soul, including the problem-solving devices (1 Cor. 10:13). And if a believer fails, recovery is as near as the rebound technique, which is a basic problem-solving device (Job 42:6; Ps. 32:5; 1 John 1:9).[84]

Suffering has different purposes in each successive stage of spiritual growth. Note some of these purposes in the course of spiritual adulthood, which begins when the believer gains spiritual self-esteem, followed by spiritual autonomy and spiritual maturity. When a believer attains spiritual self-esteem, God consolidates his strength and protects him from self-righteousness by sending *providential preventive suffering* (2 Cor. 12:7). The believer who perseveres in utilizing his divine assets and succeeds under providential preventive suffering advances to spiritual autonomy. In spiritual autonomy he receives *momentum testing* so that he may appreciate Christ more fully and utilize the resources on which He Himself relied (Phil. 3:10). If the believer passes momentum testing, he moves into spiritual maturity. As a mature believer he has the capacity to handle the most challenging suffering in the Christian life. I designate this *evidence testing*, in which God calls him—as it were—to the witness stand as evidence for God's case in the appeal trial of Satan (Job 1:6–11; 2:1–6; cf., Matt. 4:1–11). Evidence testing is Satan's cross-examination of the witness. Under the rigors of evidence testing, the supreme efficacy of God's grace glorifies Him to the maximum on earth.[85]

---

84. Thieme, *Freedom through Military Victory*, 69–83.

85. Providential preventive suffering, momentum testing, and evidence testing are discussed in Thieme, *Christian Suffering*.

God does not administer any of these categories of suffering until the believer can handle the pressure and benefit from the experience (1 Cor. 10:13). Suffering for blessing is never designed to destroy the growing believer. God's purpose is to replace the Christian's futile confidence in human resources with increased confidence in God. The pain is real, but always the purpose is blessing. Indeed, in eternity past God graciously included suffering in the advancing believer's portfolio. Suffering for blessing is necessary to intensify his use of all other assets in his portfolio.

The believer who fails to reach spiritual self-esteem does not receive suffering assets. He still suffers, but his pain is not designed by God for blessing. Instead, his own bad decisions cause him to suffer under the law of volitional responsibility. And in the midst of self-induced misery, he may also incur divine discipline. God disciplines the believer to alert him to his failure and to motivate his return to the only solution: the protocol plan of God.

## *Personnel Assets in the Church Age Portfolio*

Having discussed primary and secondary assets in the Christian's portfolio, we turn now to the special category of assets that sustains the operation of the local church. I call them *personnel assets* because they relate the individual believer to an organization or group of believers in which he plays an important part.

Every Church Age believer possesses at least one spiritual gift (1 Cor. 12:7). Spiritual gifts are God-given talents or abilities related to the function of the royal family of God on earth. From His sovereign bounty the victorious Lord Jesus Christ initially distributed spiritual gifts to celebrate His triumph (Eph. 4:7–13). Shortly after the Church Age began, the Holy Spirit took over the distribution of spiritual gifts as part of His ministry of glorifying Christ (John 16:14). Throughout the Church Age, God the Holy Spirit sovereignly bestows spiritual gifts at the moment of salvation (1 Cor. 12:11; Heb. 2:4).

Totally apart from human merit, ability, or talent, spiritual gifts operate on divine power, not on human energy. Therefore, the spiritual gift remains unexploited until the believer has begun to grow. When he reaches spiritual adulthood, his gift functions fully and effectively, even if he is unaware that his activities involve a spiritual gift. The only gifts that demand special preparation in order to function properly are the communication gifts, particularly the gift of pastor-teacher, and certain gifts of administration.[86]

All believers have equal privilege and equal opportunity to execute the protocol plan of God, but equality ends where the secondary assets begin. These assets accrue with spiritual growth, which depends on volition. Some believers choose to advance; most do not. Furthermore, equality does not extend into the realm of personnel assets, or spiritual gifts. Spiritual gifts create differences in function within the Body of Christ (Rom. 12:4–8; 1 Cor. 12—14). The individual's spiritual gift is part of what gives him a personal destiny within the royal family of God. The fulfillment of this destiny is a Christian's unique contribution to resolving the angelic conflict.

This completes our discussion of the Church Age believer's portfolio of invisible assets. So far we have seen four characteristics that make the Church Age unique. These have been the baptism of the Holy Spirit, the protocol plan of God, mystery doctrine, and the portfolio. We now turn to a fifth characteristic.

## THE EQUALITY FACTOR

Election and predestination are tremendous advantages to the Church Age believer. They deserve special attention because they are the *equality factor*. Every member of the royal family of God has equal privilege and equal opportunity to execute the protocol plan of God. At the moment of salvation, no one is superior; no one is inferior. No one has a higher position than any other, and no one is disadvantaged. All the human standards of superiority and inferiority are set aside by the election and predestination of each Church Age believer in eternity past. Race, gender, intelligence, nationality, economic situation, social standing—none of these help or hinder the believer in fulfilling the protocol plan of God. *Help* lies entirely in divine assets, and the only *hindrance* is the believer's own refusal to learn Bible doctrine and utilize his invisible divine assets.

---

86. Thieme, *The Integrity of God*, 105–06; *Tongues*, 45–46, 49.

Specific aspects of election and predestination provide equal privilege and opportunity to execute the plan of God. Under the computer asset of election, the universal priesthood gives the believer equal privilege with every other Church Age believer (Eph. 1:4).[87] Every member of the royal family represents himself before God. Also under election, logistical grace gives every Christian equal opportunity through life support, personal security, and the provisions necessary to learn Bible doctrine. Winners and losers alike are blessed with logistical grace.

| EQUALITY FACTOR | ELECTION | PREDESTINATION |
|---|---|---|
| Equal Privilege | *Royal Priesthood* | *Union with Christ* |
| Equal Opportunity | *Logistical Grace* | *Divine Dynasphere* |

Under the computer asset of predestination, union with Christ gives every believer equal privilege at the moment of salvation (Eph. 1:5). All Church Age believers have the same position in Christ through the baptism of the Holy Spirit. Also under predestination, the divine dynasphere gives every believer equal opportunity to advance by executing the protocol plan of God. Each Church Age believer possesses his own operational divine dynasphere. The divine dynasphere is the believer's royal palace, his magnificent but invisible seat of power.

Note well that equal privilege and equal opportunity for every Church Age believer in time means *inequality* in the eternal state. Each believer's volition accepts or rejects the provisions of divine sovereignty. The ROM chips (sovereignty of God) provide equality, but the PROM chips (free will of man) also function in the computer and express individuality. Some believers respond to Bible doctrine, advance spiritually, and become spiritual winners. Others reject doctrine and become spiritual losers. A Roman maxim applies to the loser: *Qui non proficit deficit.* "He who does not advance retrogresses." But another maxim pertains to the winner: *Vincit qui patitur.* "He is a winner

---

87. See pages 124–26.

who perseveres." The Christian winner keeps on using his privileges and opportunities.

## ROYAL COMMISSIONS

Among the many benefits of spiritual royalty, two divine commissions have been granted to every Church Age believer. Each Christian is a royal priest and a royal ambassador.

A priest is a human being who represents himself or others before God. In the Dispensation of the Gentiles, the head of the household represented the family in matters of worship. The family priest's duties included presenting revealed doctrine and officiating in rituals and animal sacrifices (Gen. 4:3–5; 8:20; 14:18; 22:13). In the Dispensation of Israel, God ordained the Levitical priesthood to serve on behalf of the nation (Lev. 8; Num. 3:5–10). This specialized priesthood taught Bible doctrine verbally and ceremonially through the rituals authorized in the Mosaic Law. The Levitical priesthood included only unblemished adult males from the family of Aaron in the tribe of Levi (Lev. 21:17–21).

In previous dispensations, membership in the priesthood was severely restricted. Priests were a small minority among believers. The Church Age is unique in that the priesthood has been extended to include *every* believer (1 Pet. 2:5, 9; Rev. 1:6; 5:10). In union with Christ, every Church Age believer belongs to the most exalted of all priestly orders under the high priesthood of the resurrected Jesus Christ (Heb. 9:11–14).

As a royal priest, each Church Age believer represents himself before God (Rom. 12:1; Eph. 6:7–8; Heb. 13:15–16). This is the basis for the believer's spiritual privacy, in which he lives his own life before the Lord (Rom. 14:4, 10; 2 Thess. 3:11–12). The believer's priesthood is also grounds for offering effective prayer.[88] Furthermore, the faithful intake of Bible doctrine, which is the basis for spiritual growth and the attainment of spiritual adulthood, is a priestly function. Spiritual growth is a *result* of the believer-priest's protocol function before God. The setting for the royal priest's duties is inside the divine dynasphere, in contrast to the service of earlier priesthoods at physical altars or in material temples. Although the believer is a

---

88. Thieme, *Prayer* (2003).

fully ordained priest at the moment of salvation, his priesthood becomes more effective as he attains successive stages of spiritual growth.

The universal priesthood of the Church does not imply total independence of believers from one another. The priesthood and spiritual gifts create a balance. The priesthood emphasizes the individual; spiritual gifts emphasize the group. Spiritual gifts are divinely given abilities that support the many necessary functions within the local congregation as well as outside the local church in propagating the Gospel. Believers as priests have responsibilities both before God and among other believers.

Every Christian is a priest, but not every priest has the same spiritual gifts. The gift of pastor-teacher, for example, enables a believer to accurately study and teach the Word of God. These functions belonged to the priesthoods of earlier dispensations, but in the Church Age not every priest has a gift of communicating the truth to assembled groups. All believers are royal priests, but only some royal priests are pastors. Pastors depend on the attendance of hearers. Those who are not pastors remain dependent on a pastor's exposition of the Scriptures. Although autonomous before God, believers do not live in isolation from one another.

The Christian service of individual believer-priests also brings them into contact with other Christians. Here the privacy of the priesthood treats each individual with respect and precludes sins like gossip, judging, and intolerance. This respect for the individual permits relationships to develop on a solid foundation of personal virtue. In other words, privacy contributes to rewarding relationships with other people; it is not a barrier that excludes others from the believer's life.

Each believer-priest is responsible for residing in the divine dynasphere, learning Bible doctrine, and living his own life before the Lord, but he does not have to eliminate or distort human relationships to do so. The local church is a place where believers meet to hear Bible doctrine, and wonderful human relationships can develop on the common ground of love for the Word of God. Privacy allows each person in the congregation to choose his own activities—within and outside the church—and to pursue or decline relationships on his own initiative.

The Christian's second royal warrant operates not toward God but toward man. As a royal ambassador every Church Age believer represents the Lord Jesus Christ to mankind on earth (2 Cor. 5:20; Eph. 6:20; Philemon 9).

A close analogy exists between a nation's senior diplomat to a foreign country and the Church Age believer as God's royal ambassador to man. A nation's ambassador does not appoint himself; likewise, God appoints the royal ambassador to be His representative on earth. An ambassador does not support himself; similarly, God supplies all the logistical grace necessary to perpetuate the believer's physical and spiritual life in the devil's world. An ambassador's instructions are given to him in writing; the royal ambassador operates according to the written mystery doctrines of the New Testament. An ambassador is not a citizen of the country in which he serves; the ambassador of Jesus Christ has his citizenship in heaven (Phil. 3:20). An ambassador does not reside in his assigned country to advance his own personal interests; the royal ambassador lives to glorify Christ and personally benefits not by following his own agenda but through fulfilling his royal warrant. An ambassador does not take insults personally; the believer does not regard the negative volition of mankind as a personal insult but continues to faithfully represent Christ regardless of insulting treatment by others. The recall of an ambassador accompanies a declaration of war; when the royal family is removed from the earth at the Rapture, the violent Tribulation will commence as the next dispensation.

# THE INDWELLING OF THE TRINITY

## *God Residing in the Believer*

Never before the Church Age and never afterward does God indwell every believer's body. At the moment of salvation, the Father, the Son, and the Holy Spirit take up residence in the body of the Church Age believer. God's indwelling continues uninterrupted throughout the believer's life. Scripture documents this unprecedented indwelling:

1. *The indwelling of God the Father* (John 14:23; Eph. 4:6; 2 John 9).

2. *The indwelling of God the Son* (John 14:20; 17:22–23, 26; Rom. 8:10; 2 Cor. 13:5; Gal. 2:20; Col. 1:27; 1 John 2:23–24).
3. *The indwelling of God the Holy Spirit* (Rom. 8:11; 1 Cor. 3:16; 6:19–20; 2 Cor. 6:16).

How can God indwell a believer's body? God is omnipresent, which involves His immanence and His transcendence (Deut. 4:39; 1 Kings 8:27; Ps. 139:7–8; Prov. 15:3; Isa. 57:5). *Immanence* means His entire essence is always present everywhere so that the whole of God is in every place (Jer. 23:23–24; Acts 17:27–28). *Transcendence* means He is independent of the created universe so that no particular place exclusively contains Him (Ps. 113:5–6; Isa. 55:8–9; John 8:23). Immanence and transcendence exist in balance, so that "the whole earth is full of His glory" (He is wholly in every point in the universe), while at the same time He is "holy" and "lofty and exalted" infinitely beyond the universe (Isa. 6:1–3). If God is everywhere, what is the meaning of His special indwelling of the Church Age believer's body?

The combination of immanence and transcendence means that God is free to be local, to have a presence at a particular location (Ex. 19:20; 24:9–18; 40:34; Lev. 16:2; John 1:14). And since He is not restricted to time and space, He can decide *how* He wants to dwell in these temporal and physical dimensions. He does not always have to be present in the same sense. When He dwells within creation, therefore, He dwells by His own choice and in a manner of His own choosing. His sovereign decision in this matter is a striking expression of His love and His eternal purpose.

The indwelling of the Church Age believer's body is God's local presence in a more intimate relationship with the believer than has ever existed prior to this dispensation. God's personal, indwelling presence within the Christian's body is an astounding fact and the basis for blessings beyond imagination.

## The Indwelling of the Father

Each member of the Trinity has a purpose for residing in the believer's body. The indwelling of the Father is related to the glorification of His protocol plan (Eph. 1:3, 6, 12). The Father is the author of our portfolio of invisible assets. He is the grantor of our escrow blessings for time and eternity. He is the mastermind of the protocol plan for the Church Age. He is the designer of the divine dynasphere, the invisible sphere of power in which the protocol plan is executed.

The Father is not the revealed member of the Trinity; the Lord Jesus Christ is. The Father is not the divine agent in the believer's execution of the Christian way of life; the Holy Spirit is. Because God the Father is revealed indirectly—through Christ by the power of the Spirit—little appears in Scripture concerning His personal indwelling. The Bible presents only the arresting fact that He does indeed indwell every Church Age believer. His indwelling guarantees His personal ministry to every believer.

## The Indwelling of Jesus Christ

*Shekinah Glory* was originally a Jewish theological term for the presence of God made manifest. *Shekinah* comes from the Hebrew word שָׁכַן (*shakan*) meaning "to dwell." The Son is the revealed member of the Godhead (John 1:18), the special divine presence, or *shekinah*, who is *glorified* among men. The Lord Jesus Christ is the Shekinah Glory.

The Shekinah Glory appears in numerous dispensations, establishing a continuity from age to age. But the change of residence of the Shekinah Glory is yet another example of the dramatic differences between the dispensations. In the Dispensation of Israel, the preincarnate Christ took the form of a pillar of fire and smoke that led and defended the Jews (Ex. 13:21–22; 14:19; 16:7, 10; 24:16–17). The Shekinah Glory also dwelt between the golden cherubs in the Tabernacle and later in Solomon's Temple as a sign of blessing for the nation of Israel (Lev. 26:11–12; cf., Ex. 25:22; 33:9–10; 40:34–38; Lev. 9:23; Num. 16:42; 1 Kings 8:11; 2 Chron. 5:13*b*–14).

In the Dispensation of the Hypostatic Union, the revealed member of the Godhead "became flesh and dwelt [tabernacled] among us and we beheld His glory [the Shekinah Glory] . . . full of grace and truth" (John 1:14). In this well-known statement John refers to the Transfiguration (Matt. 17:1–8; Mark 9:2–8; Luke 9:28–56), in which he witnessed the glory of Christ's deity briefly revealed. During the

Transfiguration the Voice declared that Christ is the revelation of the Father (John 6:46; 14:9–10), the very Shekinah Glory that appeared in Isaiah's vision of the enthroned Lord "lofty and exalted, with the train of His robe filling the temple" (Isa. 6:1; John 12:37–41). The Old Testament Shekinah Glory in the Tabernacle and Temple and the incarnate Christ are the same Person. Earlier our Lord had referred to His body as a temple (John 2:18–22), the new dwelling place of the Shekinah Glory. The Shekinah Glory had changed residence from the Temple to the body of Jesus Christ. The incarnate Christ is the "flashing forth of [God's] glory" (Heb. 1:3).[89]

In the Church Age, the body of each believer is a temple in which Jesus Christ, the Shekinah Glory, dwells (2 Cor. 6:16; cf., Lev. 26:12). This change of residence of the Shekinah Glory indicates the transition between the Dispensation of the Hypostatic Union and the Dispensation of the Church. The indwelling of God the Son in the body of the Church Age believer is the escutcheon or badge of the royal family.

The Shekinah Glory has fulfilled different purposes in God's plan for different dispensations. Under the ritual plan of God in Israel, the Shekinah Glory dwelt in the Tabernacle and Temple to be the focal point of worship in the nation. The Shekinah Glory resided *among* His people but not *in* them. The indwelling of the Shekinah Glory within individual believers was a concept totally unknown to the Jews. Under the incarnation plan of God, the purpose of the Shekinah Glory in human body was to provide salvation. Jesus Christ came in the flesh to bear man's sins in His body on the cross (1 Pet. 2:24). Under the protocol plan for the Church, the Shekinah Glory indwells every believer's body for the purpose of reflecting the glory of Christ. By advancing to spiritual maturity, the Church Age believer is "transformed into the same image" and glorifies Christ in his body (1 Cor. 6:19–20).

Every member of the royal family is a new spiritual species permanently indwelt by Christ. The indwelling Christ never leaves the Church Age believer (Col. 1:27), unlike the Shekinah Glory's poignant, reluctant departure from apostate Israel (1 Sam. 4:21; Ezek. 9:3; 10:4, 18; 11:22–23). This permanent status, along with the ministry of

---

89. R. B. Thieme III, "The Panorama of the Shekinah Glory" (Th.M. Thesis, Western Conservative Baptist Seminary, Portland, Oregon, 1987).

God the Holy Spirit, gives the Church Age believer unprecedented op-opportunity for spiritual impact.

> Now the Lord is the Spirit [deity of the Holy Spirit], and where the Spirit of the Lord is, there is freedom [freedom to mature]. Now we all, with an unveiled face [the filling of the Spirit gives spiritual perception] looking into a mirror [Bible doctrine, the mind of Christ] to produce a reflection [a reflection of Christ, who indwells us], namely, the glory of the Lord [the Shekinah Glory revealed to us by the Holy Spirit, who illuminates Bible doctrine (John 16:13–14)], are being transformed into the same image [the execution of the protocol plan of God manifests in us the glory of Christ] from glory to glory [from the source, the in-dwelling Shekinah Glory, to the manifestation of the Shekinah Glory in the Church Age believer who fol-lows the protocol plan], as it were, from the Spirit of the Lord [the power of the Holy Spirit which executes the protocol plan]. (2 Cor. 3:17–18)

As in previous dispensations, the Shekinah Glory is both a sign and a guarantee of blessing. Jesus Christ's presence in the Church Age believer assures him that his portfolio of invisible assets is now avail-able. The indwelling Jesus Christ is the escrow officer. He Himself is the depositary with whom the Father entrusted escrow blessings for time and eternity (Eph. 1:3). His presence in the believer's body guar-antees that these irrevocable blessings *will* be distributed if he attains spiritual maturity through execution of the protocol plan.

Christ's indwelling of the body is also an assurance of eternal life in the presence of God. At death the believer departs from the body and comes "face-to-face with the Lord" in heaven (2 Cor. 5:8). Christ is personally invisible while indwelling the believer's mortal body (1 Pet. 1:8). He becomes visible in the moment of death. The doctrine of the indwelling of Christ takes the fear out of death, for the Lord who even now indwells the believer will be the first Person he will see.

These guarantees and assurances encourage the believer while he remains on earth to execute the protocol plan of God. The Church Age believer's confidence can surpass even the confidence of David who wrote, "Even though I walk through the valley of the shadow of death, I fear no evil; for Thou art with me" (Ps. 23:4). The same Lord who was *with* the heroes of the Old Testament dwells *in* every Church Age believer (John 14:17–20).

While instilling confidence, the indwelling Lord Jesus Christ simultaneously becomes the object of the believer's love. The personal, indwelling presence of Christ is a compelling reason for giving priority to relationship with God over relationships with people or things. First priority goes to assimilating Bible doctrine, called the "mind of Christ" (1 Cor. 2:16), so that the believer can experience occupation with Christ. Occupation with Christ is the mature believer's constant awareness of the One he loves.

## The Indwelling of the Holy Spirit

Like the Father and the Son, God the Holy Spirit also indwells the body of every Church Age believer. The Spirit indwells to make the Christian's body a temple worthy of Christ, the Shekinah Glory (1 Cor. 3:16; 2 Cor. 6:16). The believer himself is incapable of providing an acceptable dwelling place for Christ. The sin nature inherited from fallen Adam contaminates the body throughout the believer's temporal life. Only the "washing of regeneration and renewing by the Holy Spirit" (Titus 3:5) make the "temple" fit for Christ to occupy. The existence of this inner sanctuary for Christ makes it possible (in fact, makes it even conceivable) for the believer to obey the command to "glorify God in your body" (1 Cor. 6:19–20).

This command is fulfilled by the Holy Spirit. He executes the plan of the Father in the life of the positive believer, the believer who adheres to divine protocol. Two postsalvation ministries of the Spirit are involved: indwelling and filling. The Spirit *indwells* the body so Christ may take up royal residence there, while the *filling* of the Spirit enables the believer to reflect the glory of the resident Christ (John 16:14; 2 Cor. 3:18). *Indwelling* is permanent; *filling* is intermittent. Scripture never commands the Church Age believer to be indwelt by the Spirit but rather regards His indwelling as a constant reality. The Bible does, however, command the believer to "be filled with the Spirit" (Eph. 5:18; cf., Gal. 5:16).

The Christian cannot change the indwelling of the Holy Spirit; the indwelling of the Spirit is not affected by sin. But the filling of the Spirit is a matter of choice. The believer loses the filling of the Spirit by committing sin. He restores the filling of the Spirit by confessing, or acknowledging, his sin to the Father (1 John 1:9). The principle of rebound remains the same in all dispensations as the only means of recovering fellowship with God, but fellowship with God does not include the filling of the Spirit in every dispensation.[90]

At the moment of salvation when the Spirit fills every believer, a perpetual inner conflict begins which will continue throughout the believer's life on earth.[91] The Holy Spirit and the sin nature compete for control of the soul (Eph. 3:16–17; cf., Rom. 7:15—8:13; Gal. 5:17–26). The believer's volition decides the issue: to sin or to resist temptation, to remain in a state of carnality after committing a sin or

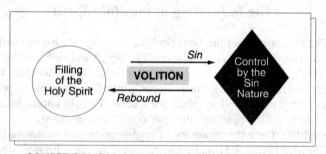

COMPETITION FOR CONTROL OF THE BELIEVER'S SOUL

to rebound, regain the filling of the Holy Spirit, and again reside in the divine dynasphere.

The filling of the Holy Spirit is the power source in the divine dynasphere. Living outside the divine dynasphere, under the power of the sin nature, is "grieving" or "quenching" the Spirit (Eph. 4:30; 1 Thess. 5:19). For the Christian, living in the divine dynasphere always implies being filled with the Holy Spirit. When the believer concentrates on Bible doctrine when it is taught, reflects upon it, or

---

90. See page 133. See also Thieme, *Rebound & Keep Moving!*; *Isolation of Sin* (2000).
91. Thieme, *Old Sin Nature vs. Holy Spirit*.

applies it in solving problems, the Holy Spirit illuminates the truth
(1 Cor. 2:9–16).

## THE AVAILABILITY OF DIVINE POWER

During Old Testament dispensations the power of God was available to a few believers. The temporary enduement of the Holy Spirit
empowered particular Old Testament believers who held positions of
unusual responsibility. God gave these prominent believers access to
His power to carry out their particular functions (Num. 11:16–17;
27:8–20; Judges 3:10; 6:34; 11:29; 13:25; 14:6; 15:14; 1 Sam.
10:6–10; 11:6; 16:13; Ezek. 2:2; 3:24; Micah 3:8; Zech. 7:12). In dramatic contrast to previous dispensations, the protocol plan of God is
executed through a power structure available to *every* Church Age
believer. The filling of the Spirit is extended to every member of the
royal family. The 'ordinary believer' is extraordinary in this dispensation.

The omnipotence of God the Holy Spirit enables the individual believer to execute the protocol plan of God. Operating the divine dynasphere, the Spirit supplies the power necessary for perception and application of Bible doctrine by which the believer advances to spiritual
maturity (John 14:16–17; 16:12–14; 1 Cor. 2:9–16).

Each Church Age believer also has available to him the power of
God the Father and God the Son. Each Person of the Trinity exercises
His absolute power on behalf of the Church Age believer. How does
this magnificent resource become operational in the believer's life? It
does so according to the mandates of divine protocol.

The omnipotence of God the Father is related to the portfolio of invisible assets. As the believer learns and obeys the Father's plan, he
begins to experience the "riches of His grace" (Eph. 1:7–9). The omnipotence of God the Son preserves the universe and perpetuates the
human race (Col. 1:17; Heb. 1:3). He controls human history by blessing nations that have a large enough pivot of positive believers and by
judging nations with too large a spinoff of negative believers. The
final two characteristics of the Church Age—concerning prophecy and
invisible heroes—explain how the Son's power operates uniquely toward the Church.

# THE ABSENCE OF PROPHECY

Unlike all other dispensations, the postcanon Church Age is the only era in which no biblical prophecy will be fulfilled. The only prophetic events concerning the Church Age are its beginning, which was prophesied by Christ (John 14:16–17; 16:7–15; Acts 1:5), and its termination at the Resurrection, or Rapture (1 Cor. 15:51–55; Phil. 3:21; 1 Thess. 4:13–18). And the only prophecies fulfilled in the precanon Church Age deal not with the Church but with Israel, whose national discipline culminated in A.D. 70.

Jesus Christ is the key to the divine interpretation of history, including past, present, and future (or prophetic) history (Eph. 3:10). In His timeless deity He knows the future as clearly as the past or present. The Bible, as the mind of Christ, is not a complete 'history book' of the future. The relatively few future events it describes are selected to reveal Christ, for "the testimony of Jesus is the spirit of prophecy" (Rev. 19:10). Many prophecies have been fulfilled in the past, just as others will be in the future. For example, the doctrines of Christ as Savior (Christology) and of His saving work (soteriology) were prophetic during the Age of the Gentiles and the Age of Israel. They were fulfilled during the Dispensation of the Hypostatic Union. Now, during the Church Age, we look back upon historical facts in connection with these doctrines. Like prophesies already fulfilled, those concerning the future reveal Christ—and the events surrounding His second advent, His reign on earth, and His eternal glorification.

The Church Age stands between two periods rich in prophecy. The Dispensation of the Hypostatic Union fulfilled many Old Testament prophecies, and the two eschatological dispensations, the Tribulation and Millennium, are described throughout the Old and New Testaments. But the Church Age is a period of prophetic silence. No events of this dispensation are found in prophecy, except for its termini.

The next scheduled prophetic events, following the Rapture, concern the Tribulation. But none of the geopolitical alignments prophesied for the Tribulation need to exist prior to the Rapture of the Church. If world conditions during the Church Age seem to parallel biblical descriptions of the Tribulation, this does not indicate that the

Rapture is near. *Throughout* the Church Age the doctrine of the immi-
nence of the Rapture holds true (James 5:8; Rev. 22:7, 12, 20). This
means the resurrection of the Church is the next prophetic event, but
the time is simply not announced. The Rapture could have occurred in
Paul's day or yesterday or may take place a thousand years from now.
Speculation by Christians has no biblical foundation and only hinders
spiritual momentum. Naturally, the growing believer's love for Christ
creates eager anticipation of His appearance (1 Cor. 1:4–8; Titus
2:13), but that enthusiasm must be tempered by patience (James
5:7–8) and redirected toward fulfilling God's purpose in this present
dispensation.[92]

When one acknowledges that the Church Age is a mystery dispensation, absent from Old Testament prophecy, he recognizes that God's
yet-unfulfilled prophecies and promises concerning Israel still belong
to Israel. In other words, the Church does not usurp the position of Israel in God's plan for the ages. God *will* keep His promises to the
Jews. In the meantime, the fulfillment of divine prophecy will not be
seen again until the Church departs and the Tribulation begins.

Why this absence of prophecy in the Church Age? Why the dramatic silence? Jesus Christ controls history, but rather than fixing our
attention on particular prophesied events, He directs us to concentrate
on the tremendous doctrines of the mystery. The "testimony of Jesus"
during this dispensation is manifested not through prophecy but
through the Church Age believer. The Church is the Body of Christ.
The Church is in union with Christ. The Church has access to the
same divine assets that sustained the humanity of Christ. The Church
possesses the completed canon of Scripture, given to sustain spiritual
growth which glorifies Christ. The Church is meant to be inculcated
with the mind of Christ. God excluded prophetic events from the postcanon Church Age to emphasize the dynamics of Bible doctrine in the
soul. Believers should learn the whole realm of Bible doctrine rather
than specialize in prophecy.

We do study prophecy. In fact, the final two dispensations are
entirely eschatological. But our Lord controls history in the Church

---

92. A study of the doctrine of the Rapture is presented in audio recordings available without charge as noted on page *iv*.

Age not through His immediate rule in a theocracy or by a succession of prophesied events but according to historical trends. This is illustrated by Christ's evaluation of local churches in Revelation 2—3, in which He comments on various tendencies in the congregations and warns of their consequences. The Church Age may even be called the dispensation of historical trends: As go believers, so go gentile client nations; as go client nations, so goes human history.

The absence of prophecy about historical developments during the Church Age is consistent with the separation of church and state. The influence of Church Age believers is invisible and generally indirect, whereas the Bible's yet unfulfilled prophecies frequently describe the political stage and events in the public spotlight.

Believers create the trends of history—anonymously. And in the Church Age the scope of the Christian's invisible impact is not restricted within a prophetic outline. The atmosphere of encouraging believers to take the initiative, advance spiritually, and pursue their spiritual destinies in the glorification of Christ continues to exist throughout the Church Age. From the beginning, this was the tenor of Christ's repeated encouragement to the disciples in the Upper Room Discourse. Christ kept urging them to "Ask Me *anything* in My name" (John 14:13–14; 15:16; 16:23–24, italics added), because the extent and manner of the glorification of His name in the Church are not announced in advance but are left to the positive volition of the individual believer. In other words, the scope of the Christian's influence is virtually unlimited.

The absence of prophecy emphasizes the individual believer's potential impact. Each believer influences history to an unprecedented degree, for good or ill, and consequently the Christian has a profound responsibility to grow up spiritually. This theme is in accord with the rest of Church Age doctrine: The fabulous divine resources at the command of the royal family—just waiting for positive volition—turn a brighter spotlight upon the free will of each believer than in any other dispensation.

Knowledge of doctrine helps the believer interpret events and historical trends as they occur in his own generation of the Church Age. The absence of prophecy from the Church Age, however, and the impact of the believer's decisions stress his need to grow up spiritually to the point that he can think for himself within a biblical frame of reference.

# INVISIBLE HEROES

The doctrine of dispensations shows the Church Age believer where he stands in the panorama of human history, but this doctrine also teaches him how to have an influence on history. When a Church Age believer advances to maturity, he has a positive impact.

In Old Testament dispensations God worked through visible heroes like Abraham, Moses, David, and Daniel. In the Church Age God works through invisible heroes. The difference is that *every* Church Age believer has equal privilege and equal opportunity to become an invisible hero. The positive impact of the royal family comes from the individual believer's personal execution of the protocol plan of God. As Christ distributes blessings to the mature believer, those blessings benefit the believer's periphery and his nation. The reverse also is true. God may protect and bless the nation as a means of blessing the mature believer. Therefore, the vigor of a generation and the divine blessing it enjoys spring from those believers who thrive under God's plan, not from political, social, or religious crusades to change the world.

The negative impact of the royal family also comes from the individual believer. The believer who rejects the plan of God brings suffering and divine discipline upon himself and becomes a source of adversity in his periphery and nation. Therefore, every individual Christian has a major role to play in his generation of the Church Age. Believers can be invisible heroes or invisible villains, but there are no ordinary Christians in the royal family of God.

The great power experiment of the Church Age was designed to create invisible heroes. An invisible hero is any Christian who advances to spiritual maturity. In maturity he has fivefold impact.

1. *Personal impact.* Individuals in the mature believer's periphery, including family, loved ones, and the organizations to which he belongs, receive blessing by their association with him.

2. *Historical impact.* The client nation receives blessing through the mature believers who reside within its borders. The vigor, prosperity, and survival of the client nation revolve around mature believers. This is the principle of the pivot (1 Kings 19:18; Matt. 5:13–16; Rom. 11:2–5; Eph. 1:21–23). A pivot of anonymous, unsung, invisible heroes is the spiritual solution to national degeneracy. Below a certain level of national decline, the spiritual pivot is the *only* solution and a nation's only hope. Blessing to the nation is an escrow blessing our Lord distributes to the mature believer. In this way Jesus Christ earns all the glory, and His reputation is not obscured by the questionable judgment of over-zealous Christians attempting to play power politics in His name. Those who vainly strive to establish the kingdom of God on earth during the Church Age overlook this principle of invisible historical impact. As a good citizen (made better by his Christianity) the believer contributes positively to his nation; he does not crusade *in the name of Christianity* to remake his nation in the image of his personal faith (Rom. 13:1–7).

3. *International impact.* Nonclient nations are blessed by association with mature believers who come as missionaries from a client nation. This is one of the responsibilities of the client nation. Unfortunately, not all missionaries are mature believers, but the missionary who *is* an invisible hero is a source of blessing to two nations: the nation in which he serves and the nation from which he is sent.

4. *Angelic impact.* God summons the invisible hero to the witness stand, as it were, to provide testimony in the appeal trial of Satan. Angels constantly observe the human race (1 Cor. 4:9; Eph. 3:10; 1 Tim. 5:21; cf., 1 Pet. 1:12), and mature believers are strong evidence of the grace of God. The devil cross-examines the mature believer through suffering (Job 1:6–12; 2:1–6; cf., Matt. 4:1–11; Eph. 6:11–12). By using divine resources to pass evidence testing, the invisible hero has far-reaching, unseen impact among the angels (1 Cor. 4:9; Eph. 3:10).[93]

---

93. Thieme, *Christian Suffering*, 158–98.

5. *Heritage impact.* The loved ones and close friends of the mature believer receive blessing after his death. David presents this encouraging principle, making this blessing an example of continuity through the dispensations (Ps. 37:25). The mature Christian can face death with complete assurance that God will care for those he leaves behind. His survivors are blessed not necessarily because they are spiritual winners themselves but because of God's high regard for the departed mature believer. Indeed, spiritual losers and even unbelievers can receive heritage impact just as they can receive personal impact during the mature Christian's lifetime.

Today the Christian's privilege of having impact as an invisible hero is being infringed. Many ministers neglect their responsibility to teach their listeners Bible doctrine but instead goad them to become involved in emotionalism, personality cults, church programs, social work, or political activism. Trends in Protestant Christianity show signs of an imbalance that emphasizes the visible at the expense of the invisible, the material at the expense of the spiritual, the believer's overt image at the expense of the inner dynamics of Bible doctrine in the soul.

This problem takes root in ignorance of dispensations. The overwhelming majority of Christians do not know what God has provided for them or why He has given them so much. After salvation, what? What does God desire the Christian to do? If believers do not realize that they belong to the royal family, how can they fulfill their destinies? How can they execute the protocol plan of God for the Church Age if they do not know such a plan exists? Ignorance undercuts every good intention. No matter how a Christian desires to make his life count for God, if he is ignorant of God's plan, he fails to glorify God. At best, the impact of his life is fleeting, no sooner achieved than dissipated. At worst, his impact is for evil as he inadvertently struggles in Satan's cause to improve the devil's world.

*Chapter Seven*

# EPILOGUE

## AFTER SALVATION, WHAT?

THE PROTESTANT REFORMERS DISSENTED from the Roman Catholic Church over several essential points of doctrine. The Reformation clarified the issue of justification by faith, but none of the Reformers—not Luther, Calvin, nor Zwingli—gave a lucid description of the believer's postsalvation way of life. Salvation is by faith in Christ; but after salvation, what?

The mechanics of the Christian way of life are no clearer to Christians today than in the darkness of late medieval Roman Catholicism. Emotionalism and empty ritualism dominate many churches. Mysticism supplants objective knowledge of Bible doctrine. Good deeds are touted as an approach to God. Morality is distorted into legalistic asceticism and is preached as a substitute for Christian virtue. Christian service is enforced through guilt, fear, penance, doubt concerning one's eternal status, or false hope of divine blessings. Political activism precludes divine viewpoint thinking. And there are endless schemes to raise money.

These age-old practices—which the Reformation did not eradicate—squander the riches that God has given to every Church Age believer. The legalism that emerged from the Reformation may differ in specifics from Roman Catholic legalism, but it is just as ineffective in defining postsalvation Christian experience.

The doctrine of dispensations is among the basic doctrines that every believer must comprehend. This doctrine enables us to recognize the biblical mechanics of the Christian way of life. Dispensations clarify the truth that the humanity of Christ established the pattern for us. Jesus is the "author and perfecter of our doctrine" (Heb. 12:2). He pioneered the protocol plan of God. He tested and proved the prototype of the divine dynasphere.

Christ was able to fulfill His destiny because He utilized the enabling power of God the Holy Spirit: "through the eternal Spirit [He] offered Himself without blemish to God" (Heb. 9:14). Christ persevered and succeeded because He applied divine problem-solving devices, illustrated by sharing the happiness of God: "because of the previously demonstrated happiness [He] endured the cross" (Heb. 12:2*b*). The assets used by Jesus Christ belonged to the prototype divine dynasphere.

Designed by the Father (John 15:10) and energized by the Holy Spirit (John 3:34), the prototype divine dynasphere was tested and proved under the most extreme pressure when Jesus Christ endured divine judgment as our substitute. After our Lord's death, the same infinite power of God that designed and energized the divine dynasphere demolished all satanic and human opposition by raising Christ from the dead and seating Him at the right hand of God (Eph. 1:19–21). Both the omnipotence of God the Father (Acts 2:24; Rom. 6:4; Eph. 1:20; Col. 2:12; 1 Thess. 1:10; 1 Pet. 1:21) and the omnipotence of God the Holy Spirit (Rom. 1:4; 8:11; 1 Pet. 3:18) were agents of Christ's resurrection.

Now *we* can live in "the power of His resurrection" (Phil. 3:10).

Divine omnipotence and divine problem-solving devices are now found in the operational divine dynasphere, which belongs to every Church Age believer (John 14:15–17; 16:13–14; 1 Cor. 6:19–20). We are commanded to "put on the Lord Jesus Christ" (Rom. 13:14), to have "Christ . . . formed" in us (Gal. 4:19), to have "Christ at home" in our hearts (Eph. 3:16–17), to "exalt [Christ]" in our bodies (Phil. 1:20–21).

The plan of God for the Church Age believer is a supernatural plan that demands a supernatural means of execution. The infinite power of God, therefore, goes silently into effect in our lives when we follow the mandates of His protocol plan. This system of divine power, available only to the Church, can handle any difficulty in our lives and will glorify Christ as in no other dispensation.

WE ARE UNITED FOREVER with Christ. The Trinity indwells our bodies. In the face of these astonishing truths, we ask with profound reverence, "After salvation, what?"

We must learn Bible doctrine. Church Age doctrine sets forth the protocol of Christ's royal family. In mystery doctrine we learn of the portfolio God established personally for each of us in eternity past. The portfolio contains outright gifts from God that define the scope of our freedom and responsibility. We are the aristocrats of heaven residing on earth. We are royal priests. We are royal ambassadors. We have an unprecedented opportunity to utilize divine power, and God stands ready to enlarge our already vast resources.

If we learn, understand, and apply His Word, He will stimulate our own desire to know Him, lead us into eternally meaningful service, and lift us above our sufferings. He will create an impact with our lives that will resound throughout time and eternity. Our royal destiny is to become invisible heroes in the most intense and challenging dispensation in human history.

# *Scripture Index*

## OLD TESTAMENT

### GENESIS

| | |
|---|---|
| 1—3:6 | 22 |
| 1:26–28 | 23 |
| 1:28 | 25 |
| 1:29–30 | 25 |
| 2:17 | 24 |
| 2:18 | 23 |
| 2:19–20 | 23 |
| 2:20 | 23 |
| 2:23 | 23 |
| 3:7—11:32 | 24 |
| 3:8 | 22, 24 |
| 3:11–19 | 23 |
| 3:15 | 24, 25, 30 |
| 3:16 | 23 |
| 3:20 | 24 |
| 3:21 | 24 |
| 4:3–5 | 124 |
| 4:4 | 24 |
| 4:8 | 25 |
| 6:1–7 | 25 |
| 6:3 | 113 |
| 8:20 | 24, 124 |
| 8:20–22 | 25 |
| 9:1 | 25 |
| 9:3 | 25 |
| 9:8–17 | 25 |
| 9:26 | 30 |
| 10:32 | 25 |
| 11:1–9 | 25 |
| 11:8 | 26 |
| 11:31 | 26 |
| 12:1–3 | 31 |
| 12:1–4 | 26 |
| 12:2–3 | 29 |
| 12:3 | 34, 56 |
| 13:15 | 27, 31, 32 |
| 13:16 | 31 |
| 14:18 | 124 |
| 15:6 | 5, 27, 92 |
| 15:18–21 | 31 |
| 17:1–21 | 27 |
| 22:13 | 124 |
| 22:15–18 | 27, 31 |
| 26:3–5 | 27, 31 |
| 26:4 | 31 |
| 26:5 | 58 |
| 28:13–15 | 27, 31 |

28:14 ................. 31, 34
35:11 ..................... 31
35:11–12 ................. 27
35:12 ..................... 31

### EXODUS

3—4 ...................... 29
6:2–8 .................... 31
6:2–9 ................. 31, 32
6:4 ...................... 31
6:8 ...................... 31
9:16 ..................... 42
10 ...................... 128
12 ....................... 30
13:21–22 ............... 128
14:19 .................. 128
16:7 .................... 128
19 ....................... 57
19:3 ..................... 57
19:3–6 ................... 32
19:5 ..................... 58
19:5–6 ................... 34
19:20 .................. 127
24:9–18 ............... 127
24:16–17 .............. 128
25:22 .................. 128
33:9–10 ............... 128
40:34 .................. 127
40:34–38 .............. 128

### LEVITICUS

8 ....................... 124
9:23 ................... 128
16:2 ................... 127
20:9 .................... 63
20:10 ................... 63
20:13 ................... 63
21:17–21 .............. 124
26 ....................... 35
26:11–12 .............. 128

26:12 .................. 129
26:46 ................... 57

### NUMBERS

3:5–10 ................. 124
11:16–17 .............. 133
16:42 .................. 128
17—18 ................. 107
23:19 ................... 81
27:8–20 ............... 133
34:1–12 ................ 31

### DEUTERONOMY

4:6–8 ................ 29, 34
4:8 ..................... 31
4:32 .................... 64
4:37 ................... 107
4:39 ................... 127
7:6 .................... 107
28:1–14 ................ 33
30:1–9 ................. 31
31:9–13 ................ 29
32—40 ................. 29
33:10 ................... 29

### JOSHUA

1:2–4 ................... 31
1:7–8 ................... 32
5:13–15 ................ 29

### JUDGES

3:10 ................... 133
6:34 ................... 133
11:29 .................. 133
13:25 .................. 133
14:6 ................... 133
15:14 .................. 133

### 1 SAMUEL

4:21 ................... 129
8 ....................... 29

10:6–10 .................... 133
11:6 ...................... 133
16:13 .................... 133

## 2 SAMUEL

7:8–16 .................... 39
7:8–17 .................... 31
7:13 ...................... 32
7:16 ...................... 32

## 1 KINGS

8:11 ..................... 128
8:27 ..................... 127
19:18 .................... 138

## 2 CHRONICLES

5:13–14 ................. 128

## JOB

1:6 ....................... 73
1:6–11 ................... 120
1:6–12 ................... 138
1:12 ....................... 6
2:1 ....................... 73
2:1–6 .............. 120, 138
2:6 ........................ 6
9:2 ....................... 38
9:32–33 ................. 38
19:25–26 ......... 53, 55, 75
42:6 ..................... 120

## PSALMS

16 ........................ 76
23:4 ..................... 131
23:6 ...................... 92
32:5 ..................... 120
33:4 ...................... 81
34:15–16 ................. 67
37:25 ................... 139
46:9 ...................... 76

72 ........................ 75
72:7 ...................... 76
76:10 ..................... 42
89:20–37 ............. 31, 39
89:27–29 .................. 8
110:1 ................ 66, 87
113:5–6 ................. 127
118:22 ................... 54
138:2 ...................... 2
139:7–8 ................. 127
145:21 ..................... 6

## PROVERBS

8:30–31 ................. 112
15:3 .................... 127

## ISAIAH

2:4 ....................... 76
5:26–30 .................. 74
6:1 ...................... 129
7:14 ...................... 24
8:14–15 .................. 41
10:20–23 ................. 74
11 ........................ 75
11:6–9 .................... 76
11:9 ...................... 76
11:11–16 ................. 74
14:1–3 ................... 74
14:13–14 .................. 6
14:14 .................. 7, 72
28:11 ................ 69, 91
28:16 .................... 54
34:1–6 ................... 72
35 ........................ 75
35:1–7 ................... 76
40:3–5 .................... 8
42:1 .................... 107
45:4 .................... 107
55:8–9 .................. 127
57:5 .................... 127
62 ........................ 75

62:10–12 ................... 8
63:1–6 ................ 72, 74
65 ....................... 75
65:20 .................... 76
65:25 .................... 76

### JEREMIAH

23:23–24 ............... 127
30:4–8 ................... 72
30:7 ..................... 72
31:31–34 ............... 31
31:33–34 ............... 76
31:34 ................... 32
32:36–44 ............... 31

### EZEKIEL

2:2 ..................... 133
3:24 .................... 133
9:3 ..................... 129
10:4 .................... 129
11:16–21 ............... 31
11:22–23 ............... 129
20:34–38 ............... 75
28:16–18 ................ 6
36:21–38 ............... 31
38—39 .................. 72

### DANIEL

9:24 .................... 74
9:24–27 ................. 72
9:27 .................... 72
11:40–45 ............... 72

### HOSEA

2:18 .................... 76
4:6 ................. 34, 35

### JOEL

2:16—3:21 .............. 74
2:28–29 ................. 76
4:6 ................. 34, 35
6:1–5 .................. 127
28:11 ................... 91

### AMOS

11:12 ................... 29

### JONAH

1—4 .................... 34

### MICAH

3:8 .................... 133
4:1–8 ................... 8
4:3 .................... 76
5:2–4 ................... 8

### ZECHARIAH

3:1. .................... 73
3:1–10 .................. 6
7:12 ................... 133
8:22–23 ................. 75
8:23 .................... 75
9:9–10 .................. 8
10:6–12 ................. 74
12:1–3 ................. 72
12:5–6 ................. 74
14:1–2 ................. 72
14:4–9 ................. 75
14:9 ................... 74

# NEW TESTAMENT

## MATTHEW

| | |
|---|---|
| 1:1 | 53 |
| 1:5–6 | 40 |
| 1:20–23 | 24 |
| 2:17–18 | 40 |
| 4:1 | 51 |
| 4:1–11 | 6, 120, 138 |
| 4:14–16 | 40 |
| 4:17 | 40, 41 |
| 4:23–25 | 40 |
| 5—7 | 40, 45 |
| 5:1 | 45 |
| 5:3–11 | 46 |
| 5:5 | 46 |
| 5:12 | 46 |
| 5:13–16 | 47, 138 |
| 5:17 | 8, 34, 40, 57 |
| 5:17–19 | 57 |
| 5:18 | 40, 57 |
| 5:20 | 59 |
| 5:21–48 | 59 |
| 5:37 | 46 |
| 5:39 | 47 |
| 6:1–18 | 60 |
| 6:9–13 | 47 |
| 6:10 | 46 |
| 6:25–34 | 47, 100 |
| 6:31–34 | 47 |
| 7:1–5 | 47 |
| 7:15 | 47 |
| 7:28 | 45 |
| 8—9 | 40 |
| 11:25–30 | 40 |
| 12 | 46 |
| 12:1–8 | 40 |
| 12:18 | 51 |
| 12:23 | 53 |
| 12:28 | 51 |
| 12:45 | 47 |
| 13:10–16 | 43 |

| | |
|---|---|
| 14:13–15 | 45 |
| 14:19–23 | 45 |
| 15:7 | 45 |
| 16:18 | 54 |
| 16:23 | 45 |
| 17:1–8 | 128 |
| 21:42 | 54 |
| 21:42–43 | 55 |
| 22:15–22 | 59 |
| 22:21 | 40 |
| 22:41–46 | 53 |
| 23 | 44 |
| 23:27—25:46 | 8 |
| 23:37 | 8 |
| 23:37–39 | 40 |
| 24 | 107 |
| 24—25 | 18, 40 |
| 24:3 | 8, 44 |
| 24:15 | 44 |
| 24:16 | 44 |
| 24:20 | 44 |
| 24:21 | 73 |
| 24:22 | 107 |
| 24:23 | 44 |
| 24:34 | 44 |
| 24:42—25:13 | 45 |
| 25:31–46 | 75 |
| 25:41 | 6 |
| 26:1–2 | 45 |
| 26:28 | 40 |
| 29—31 | 44 |
| 31 | 107 |

## MARK

| | |
|---|---|
| 9:2–8 | 128 |
| 12:10 | 54 |

## LUKE

| | |
|---|---|
| 1:68 | 29 |

2:14 . . . . . . . . . . . . . . . . . . . . 6
2:40 . . . . . . . . . . . . . . . . . . . . 63
2:52 . . . . . . . . . . . . . . . . . . . . 63
4:1 . . . . . . . . . . . . . . . . . . . . 51
4:14–15 . . . . . . . . . . . . . . . . . . 51
4:18 . . . . . . . . . . . . . . . . . . . . 51
8:23 . . . . . . . . . . . . . . . . . . . 127
9:28–56 . . . . . . . . . . . . . . . . . 128
13:34–35 . . . . . . . . . . . . . . . . . 41
20:17 . . . . . . . . . . . . . . . . . . . 54
21:24 . . . . . . . . . . . . . . . . . . . 7

### JOHN

1:1 . . . . . . . . . . . . . . . . . . . . 50
1:1–4 . . . . . . . . . . . . . . . . . . . 22
1:1–14 . . . . . . . . . . . . . . . . . . 37
1:12–13 . . . . . . . . . . . . . . . . . . 40
1:14 . . . . . . . . . . 50, 54, 127, 128
1:16–17 . . . . . . . . . . . . . . . . . . 56
1:18 . . . . . . . . . . . . . . 2, 50, 128
1:29 . . . . . . . . . . . . . . . . . . . . 62
2:18–22 . . . . . . . . . . . . . . . . . 129
3:16 . . . . . . . . . . . . . . . . . . . . 42
3:18 . . . . . . . . . . . . . . . . . . 24, 78
3:34 . . . . . . . . . . . . . . . . . 51, 141
3:36 . . . . . . . . . . . . . . . . . . . . 78
4:18 . . . . . . . . . . . . . . . . . . . . 51
6:46 . . . . . . . . . . . . . . . . . . . 129
7:37–39 . . . . . . . . . . . . . . . . 51, 88
7:38 . . . . . . . . . . . . . . . . . . . 100
7:39 . . . . . . . . . . . . . . . . . 13, 60
8:23 . . . . . . . . . . . . . . . . . . . 127
11:43–44 . . . . . . . . . . . . . . . . . 53
12:10 . . . . . . . . . . . . . . . . . . . 53
12:37–41 . . . . . . . . . . . . . . . . . 129
13:31–32 . . . . . . . . . . . . . . . 13, 44
13:33–34 . . . . . . . . . . . . . . . . . 44
13:34 . . . . . . . . . . . . . . . . . . . 13
14—17 . . . . . . . . 8, 12, 18, 43, 60
14:6 . . . . . . . . . . . . . . . . . . . . 5
14:9–10 . . . . . . . . . . . . . . . . . 129
14:11–12 . . . . . . . . . . . . . . . . . 88

14:12 . . . . . . . . . . . . . . . . . . . 64
14:13–14 . . . . . . . . . . . . . . . . 136
14:15–17 . . . . . . . . . . . . . . 88, 141
14:16–17 . . . . . . . . . . . . . 133, 134
14:16–19 . . . . . . . . . . . . . . . . 115
14:17 . . . . . . . . . . . . . . . . . . . 45
14:17–20 . . . . . . . . . . . . . . . . 131
14:20 . . . . . . . . . 45, 54, 86, 127
14:23 . . . . . . . . . . . . . . . . 45, 126
15:10 . . . . . . . . . 13, 70, 90, 141
15:10–11 . . . . . . . . . . . . . . . . . 51
15:10–12 . . . . . . . . . . . . . . . . . 63
15:16 . . . . . . . . . . . . . . . . . . . 136
15:18—16:4 . . . . . . . . . . . . . . . 44
16:1–2 . . . . . . . . . . . . . . . . . . . 45
16:7–15 . . . . . . . . . . . . . . . . . 134
16:12–14 . . . . . . . . . . . . . . . . 133
16:12–15 . . . . . . . . . . . . . . . . . 9
16:13–14 . . . . . 88, 114, 130, 141
16:14 . . . . . . . . . . . . 13, 121, 131
16:23–24 . . . . . . . . . . . . . . . . 136
16:32 . . . . . . . . . . . . . . . . . . . 45
17:17 . . . . . . . . . . . . . . . . . . . 88
17:20–21 . . . . . . . . . . . . . . . . . 44
17:21–23 . . . . . . . . . . . . . . . . . 45
17:22–23 . . . . . . . . . . . . . . . . 127
17:26 . . . . . . . . . . . . . . . . 45, 127

### ACTS

1:5 . . . . . . . . . . . . . . . . . . 86, 134
1:6 . . . . . . . . . . . . . . . . . . 42, 44
1:6–7 . . . . . . . . . . . . . . . . . . 7, 82
1:7 . . . . . . . . . . . . . . . . . . . 10, 12
1:8 . . . . . . . . . . . . . . . . . . . . 9, 68
2:1–4 . . . . . . . . . . . . . . . . . . . 86
2:24 . . . . . . . . . . . . . . . . . . . 141
4:10–12 . . . . . . . . . . . . . . . . 54, 55
4:12 . . . . . . . . . . . . . . . . . . . . 5
10:38 . . . . . . . . . . . . . . . . . . . 51
10:45 . . . . . . . . . . . . . . . . . . . 4
11:15–17 . . . . . . . . . . . . . . . . . 86

13:8–12 .................. 69
14:3 ..................... 69
15:5 ..................... 31
15:5–11 .................. 56
15:17 .................... 29
15:24 .................... 56
16:27–34 ................. 84
16:31 ..................... 5
17:21 .................... 26
17:23 .................... 26
17:24 .................... 54
17:25 .................... 54
17:26–27 ................. 26
17:27–28 ................ 127
17:28 .................... 26
19:11–12 ................. 69
22:28 .................... 84
24—26 ................... 84

## ROMANS

1:2–4 .................... 37
1:3 ...................... 65
1:4 ............... 51, 65, 141
1:14 ..................... 68
1:16 .................... 114
2:12–14 .................. 31
2:14–16 .................. 58
2:17–20 .................. 57
3:19 ..................... 57
3:22 ...................... 5
3:30 ...................... 5
4:1–16 ................... 25
4:17–21 .................. 27
5:8–10 ................... 62
5:17 ..................... 75
6:1–2 ..................... 2
6:3 ...................... 87
6:4 ................. 88, 141
6:4–5 .................... 87
6:14 ............. 20, 31, 56, 57
6:15 ..................... 58
7:4–6 .................... 56

7:15—8:13 ............... 132
8:2 ...................... 58
8:2–3 .................... 56
8:2–4 ................. 58, 63
8:4 ...................... 56
8:10 .................... 127
8:11 ............... 127, 141
8:16–17 ............... 92, 93
8:18 ...................... 7
8:19–21 .................. 76
8:28 ..................... 92
8:29 ..................... 87
8:29–30 ................... 2
8:30 ..................... 92
8:32 ............... 1, 3, 42
8:38–39 ............ 1, 15, 92
9:4 ...................... 57
9:6–8 .................... 32
9:17 ..................... 42
9:23 ...................... 6
9:23–24 ................... 2
9:30–33 .................. 55
9:33 ..................... 41
10 ...................... 124
10:4 ............ 34, 40, 52, 57
11:2–5 .................. 138
11:5 ...................... 7
11:5–7 .................. 107
11:25 ..................... 4
11:25–36 .................. 6
12:1 .................... 124
12:2 ............. 2, 3, 89, 114
12:3 ...................... 2
12:4–8 .................. 122
13:1–7 ......... 58, 59, 68, 138
13:4 ............... 62, 63, 68
13:11 ..................... 7
13:14 ............... 88, 141
14:4 .................... 124
14:10–13 ................. 47
16:17–18 ................. 77
16:25 ................. 7, 11

16:25–26 ............... 14, 96

### 1 CORINTHIANS

1:2 ................. 15, 86, 92
1:4–8 .................... 135
1:8 ...................... 91
1:20–31 .................. 96
1:22 ..................... 77
1:23–25 .................. 77
1:30 ............. 15, 86, 92
2:4–5 ............... 95, 112
2:5 ..................... 113
2:6–9 ................... 114
2:7 ..................... 97
2:9–16 .................. 133
2:10 .................... 112
2:10–16 ................. 114
2:12 .................... 114
2:12–14 ................. 24
2:13 .................... 114
2:16 ................. 2, 131
3:11 .................... 54
3:11–15 ............ 102, 118
3:12–15 ................. 101
3:15 .................... 103
3:16 ............... 127, 131
4:5 ..................... 101
4:9 ..................... 138
6:19–20 ..... 127, 129, 131, 141
7:19 .................... 58
9:16 .................... 68
9:17 .................... 11
9:19–21 ................. 63
9:20–21 ................. 58
9:24–27 ................. 102
10:13 ............... 120, 121
12—14 .............. 69, 122
12:7 .................... 121
12:11 ................... 121
12:12–13 ................ 86
12:13 ................... 86

13:8 ................. 69, 91
14:19 ................... 70
14:21 ................... 69
14:21–22 ................ 91
15:20 ................... 53
15:22–23 ................ 53
15:23 ................... 53
15:23–24 ................ 77
15:24 ............... 53, 75
15:51–55 ............... 134
15:54 ................... 53
15:57 ................... 66

### 2 CORINTHIANS

3:7–13 .................. 56
3:17–18 ................ 130
3:18 ................... 131
4:5 .................... 68
4:16 ................... 89
5:8 .................... 130
5:10 ................... 101
5:17 ............. 15, 28, 86
5:20 ................... 126
5:21 ................... 92
6:16 ............... 127, 131
9:7–8 .................. 3
12:7 ................... 120
13:5 ................... 127

### GALATIANS

2 ...................... 9
2:9 .................... 56
2:19 ................... 31
2:20 .............. 100, 127
3:1–5 .................. 85
3:3 .................... 113
3:6–9 .................. 25
3:14 ................... 85
3:19–25 ................ 56
3:23 ................... 93
3:23–25 ................ 57

3:25 . . . . . . . . . . . . . . . . . . . . . . 21
3:25–26 . . . . . . . . . . . . . . . . . . 93
3:26 . . . . . . . . . . . . . . . . . 25, 92
3:26–27 . . . . . . . . . . . . . . . . . 85
3:27 . . . . . . . . . . . . . . . . . . . . . 93
4:4 . . . . . . . . . . . . . . . . . . . . . . 50
4:4–5 . . . . . . . . . . . . . . . . . . . . 50
4:19 . . . . . . . . . . . . . . . . . . . . 141
5:1 . . . . . . . . . . . . . . . . . . . 59, 63
5:3–4 . . . . . . . . . . . . . . . . . . . . 57
5:5 . . . . . . . . . . . . . . . . . . . . . . 88
5:13 . . . . . . . . . . . . . . . . . . . . . 63
5:14 . . . . . . . . . . . . . . . . . . . . . 57
5:16 . . . . . . . . . . . . 88, 114, 132
5:16–26 . . . . . . . . . . . . . . . . . 114
5:17–26 . . . . . . . . . . . . . . . . . 132
5:18 . . . . . . . . . . . . . . . . . . 56, 57
5:22–23 . . . . . . . . . . . . . . . . . . 88
6:2 . . . . . . . . . . . . . . . . . . . . . . 58
6:15 . . . . . . . . . . . . . . . . . . . . . . 4

EPHESIANS

Book of . . . . . . . . . . . . . . . . . . . 68
1:3 . . . . . . 3, 97, 98, 103, 127, 130
1:3–6 . . . . . . . . . . . . . . . . . . . . 98
1:3–14 . . . . . . . . . . . . . . . . . . . 15
1:4 . . . . . . . . 91, 92, 99, 103, 123
1:4–6 . . . . . . . . . . . . . . . . . . . 104
1:5 . . . . . . . . . . . . . . 92, 93, 123
1:5–6 . . . . . . . . . . . . . . . . . . . 106
1:6 . . . . . . . . . . . . . . . . . . . . . 127
1:6–8 . . . . . . . . . . . . . . . . . . . . 97
1:8–10 . . . . . . . . . . . . . . . . . . . 11
1:9 . . . . . . . . . . . . . . . . . . . . . . 14
1:10 . . . . . . . . . . . . . . . . . . . . . 50
1:12 . . . . . . . . . . . . . . . . . . . . 127
1:13 . . . . . . . . . . . . . . . . . . . . 113
1:17–23 . . . . . . . . . . . . . . . . . . . 6
1:18 . . . . . . . . . . . . . . . . 2, 83, 97
1:18–23 . . . . . . . . . . . . . . . . . 108
1:19–21 . . . . . . . . . . . . . . . . . 141
1:20 . . . . . . . . . . . . . . . . . . . . 141

1:21–23 . . . . . . . . . . 13, 47, 138
1:22–23 . . . . . . . . . . . . . 66, 86
2:1 . . . . . . . . . . . . . . . . . . . . . 112
2:4–5 . . . . . . . . . . . . . . . . . . . 113
2:8–9 . . . . . . . . . . . . . . . . 5, 113
2:10 . . . . . . . . . . . . . . . . . . . . 117
2:11–12 . . . . . . . . . . . . . . . . . . . 7
2:11–22 . . . . . . . . . . . . . . . . 4, 56
2:15 . . . . . . . . . . . . . . . . . 52, 56
2:20 . . . . . . . . . . . . . . . . . . . . . 55
3:1–5 . . . . . . . . . . . . . . . . . . . . 14
3:1–9 . . . . . . . . . . . . . . . . . . . . 96
3:2 . . . . . . . . . . . . . . . . . . . . . . 70
3:2–3 . . . . . . . . . . . . . . . . . . . . 11
3:8 . . . . . . . . . . . . . . . . . . . . . . 97
3:8–9 . . . . . . . . . . . . . . . . . . . . 11
3:9 . . . . . . . . . . . . . . . . . . . 11, 94
3:10 . . . . . 6, 7, 77, 103, 134, 138
3:10–11 . . . . . . . . . . . . . . . . . . . 4
3:16 . . . . . . . . . . . . . . . . . . . . . 97
3:16–17 . . . . . . . . . . . . . 132, 141
3:18 . . . . . . . . . . . . . . . . . . . . . 97
3:19 . . . . . . . . . . . . . . . . . . . . . . 3
3:20 . . . . . . . . . . . . . . . . . . 83, 98
3:21 . . . . . . . . . . . . . . . . . . . . . . 6
4:1 . . . . . . . . . . . . . . . 85, 88, 107
4:4–5 . . . . . . . . . . . . . . . . . . . . 86
4:6 . . . . . . . . . . . . . . . . . . . . . 126
4:7–13 . . . . . . . . . . . . . . . . . . 121
4:8 . . . . . . . . . . . . . . . . . . . . 2, 66
4:11–13 . . . . . . . . . . . . . . . . 2, 70
4:13–16 . . . . . . . . . . . . . . . . . . . 2
4:15 . . . . . . . . . . . . . . . . . . . . . 52
4:20 . . . . . . . . . . . . . . . . . . . . 113
4:20–24 . . . . . . . . . . . . . . . . . . 95
4:21 . . . . . . . . . . . . . . . . . . . . . 95
4:22–24 . . . . . . . . . . . . . . . . . 1, 2
4:23 . . . . . . . . . . . . . . . . . 89, 113
4:24–25 . . . . . . . . . . . . . . . . . . 95
4:29 . . . . . . . . . . . . . . . . . . . . . 95
4:30 . . . . . . . 89, 95, 113, 114, 132
5:1–2 . . . . . . . . . . . . . . . . . . . . 88

5:2 . . . . . . . . . . . . . . . . . . . . . . 90
5:18 . . . . . . . . . . . 88, 114, 132
5:22–32 . . . . . . . . . . . . . . . . . 86
5:22–33 . . . . . . . . . . . . . . . . . 24
5:25–27 . . . . . . . . . . . . . . . . . 13
5:32 . . . . . . . . . . . . . . . . . . . . 81
6:7–8 . . . . . . . . . . . . . . . . . . 124
6:11–12 . . . . . . . . . . . . . . . . 138
6:12 . . . . . . . . . . . . . . . . . . . . . 7
6:20 . . . . . . . . . . . . . . . . . . . 126

### PHILIPPIANS

1:20–21 . . . . . . . . . . . . . . . . 141
1:21 . . . . . . . . . . . . . . . . . . . 100
2:1 . . . . . . . . . . . . . . . . . . . . 116
2:5 . . . . . . . . . . . . . . . . . . . 2, 3
2:5–11 . . . . . . . . . . . . . . . . . . 38
2:7–8 . . . . . . . . . . . . . . . 38, 51
2:13–16 . . . . . . . . . . . . . . . . 117
2:16 . . . . . . . . . . . . . . . . . . . 118
2:27 . . . . . . . . . . . . . . . . . . . . 69
3:12–14 . . . . . . . . . . . . . . . . 116
3:10 . . . . . . . . . . 70, 120, 141
3:14 . . . . . . . . . . . . . . . . . . . 115
3:20 . . . . . . . . . . . . . . . . . . . 126
3:21 . . . . . . . . . . . . . . . 91, 134
4:1 . . . . . . . . . . . . . . . . . . . . 102
4:2–3 . . . . . . . . . . . . . . . . . . 100
4:8 . . . . . . . . . . . . . . . . . . . . . 56
4:11–13 . . . . . . . . . . . . . . . . . 24
4:19 . . . . . . . . . . . . . . . 97, 100

### COLOSSIANS

Book of . . . . . . . . . . . . . . . . . 68
1:18 . . . . . . . . . . . . . . . . . . . . 52
1:25–27 . . . . . . . . . . . . . . . . . 15
1:25–28 . . . . . . . . . . . . . . . . . 96
1:25–29 . . . . . . . . . . . . . . . . . 11
1:26 . . . . . . . . . . . . . . . . . . . . 11
1:27 . . . . . . . . . . . 97, 127, 129
2:2 . . . . . . . . . . . . . . . . . . . . . 97

2:12 . . . . . . . . . . . . . . . 87, 141
2:16–17 . . . . . . . . . . . . . . . . . 21
2:16—3:3 . . . . . . . . . . . . . . . . . 9
2:17 . . . . . . . . . . . . . . . . . . . . 30
2:20–23 . . . . . . . . . . . . . . . . 103
3:24 . . . . . . . . . . . . . . . . . . . 103

### 1 THESSALONIANS

1:4 . . . . . . . . . . . . . . . . . . . . 107
1:10 . . . . . . . . . . . . . . . . . . . 141
2:19–20 . . . . . . . . . . . . . . . . 102
4:13–18 . . . . . . . . . . . . . . . . 134
5:1–2 . . . . . . . . . . . . . 8, 10, 82
5:4 . . . . . . . . . . . . . . . . . . . . . 10
5:19 . . . . . . . . . . . 89, 114, 132
5:23 . . . . . . . . . . . . . . . . 24, 91

### 2 THESSALONIANS

2:7 . . . . . . . . . . . . . . . . . . . . . 72
2:13 . . . . . . . . . . . . . . . . . . . 107
2:13–14 . . . . . . . . . . . . . . . . . 86
3:11–12 . . . . . . . . . . . . . . . . 124

### 1 TIMOTHY

1:3–4 . . . . . . . . . . . . . . . . . . . 11
2:5–6 . . . . . . . . . . . . . . . . . . . 38
2:15 . . . . . . . . . . . . . . . . . . . . 24
3:9 . . . . . . . . . . . . . . . . . . . . . 97
3:16 . . . . . . . . . . . . . 13, 38, 90
4:1 . . . . . . . . . . . . . . . . . . . . . 95
4:7–8 . . . . . . . . . . . . . . . . . . . 90
5:21 . . . . . . . . . . . . . . . . . . . 138
6:16 . . . . . . . . . . . . . . . . . . . . 53

### 2 TIMOTHY

2:5 . . . . . . . . . . . . . . . . 101, 103
2:13 . . . . . . . . . . . . . . . . . . . . 90
2:15 . . . . . . . . . . . . . . . . . 2, 114
2:21 . . . . . . . . . . . . . . . . . . . . 88
3:16–17 . . . . . . . . . . . . . . . . . . 2
4:5 . . . . . . . . . . . . . . . . . . . . . 68

4:7–8 .................... 101

## TITUS

2:13 .................... 135
2:14 .................... 117
3:5 .................... 131

## PHILEMON

9 ...................... 126

## HEBREWS

1:1–2 .................. 4, 64
1:1–3 .................. 22, 50
1:2 ..................... 50
1:3 .................... 129
1:3–4 ................... 66
1:4 ..................... 87
1:8 ..................... 39
1:12 .................... 39
1:13 ................. 66, 87
1:13–14 ................. 87
2:3 ..................... 60
2:4 .................... 121
2:9–11 .................. 87
2:14–15 ................. 38
3:5–6 .................... 4
4:1–10 .................. 47
4:12 ................... 114
4:16 ..................... 2
5:11 ................... 115
5:14 ................... 115
6:1 .................... 118
6:1–6 .................. 115
6:13–18 ................. 26
6:16 ................... 129
7:4–5 ................... 38
7:12 .................... 59
7:14 .................... 38
7:28 .................... 38
8:1 ..................... 59
8:1–2 ................... 54

8:5 .................... 30, 54
8:8–12 .................. 31
8:13 ......... 30, 56, 57, 58
9:11–14 ................ 124
9:13–14 ................. 88
9:14 ......... 51, 118, 141
9:15 .................... 56
10—14 ................... 38
10:1 ............. 30, 40, 77
10:5 ................. 38, 39
10:9 ............. 56, 57, 58
10:10–14 ................ 92
10:12 ................... 87
10:15–17 ................ 31
11:8–10 ................. 26
11:11–12 ................ 27
12:2 ............ 51, 56, 141
13:8 .................... 65
13:15–16 ............... 124

## JAMES

1:9–10 .................. 88
1:12 ................... 102
1:17 ..................... 3
1:22 ................... 111
4:6 .................. 3, 100
5:7–8 .................. 135
5:8 ................... 135

## 1 PETER

1:3–4 .................. 103
1:4 ................. 100, 103
1:4–5 .................... 1
1:8 .................. 3, 130
1:10–12 ................. 13
1:12 ................... 138
1:18–19 ................. 62
1:20 ..................... 7
1:21 ............... 23, 141
2:4–7 ................... 54
2:5 ................. 54, 124

2:6 ............................ 107
2:9 .................... 59, 65, 124
2:24 ........................... 129
3:18 ........................... 141
4:1 ............................ 107
5:1–4 .......................... 102
5:7 ............................. 47

### 2 PETER

1:2–4 ........................... 56
1:3 ...................... 90, 107
1:4 ............................. 88
1:11 ............................ 92
3:1–16 ........................... 9
3:7 ............................. 78
3:9 ............................. 42
3:10–13 ......................... 78
3:11 ............................ 90
3:15–16 .......................... 9
3:18 ............................. 2

### 1 JOHN

Book of ......................... 68
1:5—2:6 .......................... 2
1:8–10 .......................... 95
1:9 ............... 88, 120, 132
2:6 ....................... 70, 88
2:23–24 ........................ 127
3:1–2 ........................... 92
3:2 ............................. 91
5:11 ............................ 92
5:11–12 ......................... 92

### 2 JOHN

Book of ......................... 68
9 .............................. 126

### 3 JOHN

Book of ......................... 68

### REVELATION

1:5 ............................. 53
1:6 ............................ 124
1:8 ............................. 4
1:16 ............................ 75
2—3 ....................... 18, 68
2:10 ........................... 102
3:10 ............................ 71
5:10 ........................... 124
6—19 ............................ 18
6:1–11 .......................... 73
7:4–8 ..................... 74, 107
7:14 ............................ 73
11—15 ........................... 77
11:3 ............................ 72
11:3–13 ......................... 74
12 ............................. 135
12:6 ............................ 72
12:7–9 .......................... 73
12:12 ........................... 72
12:17 ........................... 73
14:6–7 .......................... 74
19:10 .......................... 134
20 ............. 18, 72, 75, 135
20:1–3 .......................... 75
20:4 ....................... 53, 55
20:5 ....................... 53, 55
20:7–9 .......................... 77
20:7–10 ......................... 53
20:10 ........................... 6
20:14–15 ........................ 78
20:15 ........................... 78
21—22 ........................... 18
21—22:5 ......................... 78
21:3–4 .......................... 78
21:8 ............................ 78
21:12 ........................... 27
21:22 ........................... 54
22:4–5 .......................... 78
22:7 ........................... 135
22:16 ........................... 66
22:20 .......................... 135

# Subject Index

Abel, 25

Abraham, 16, 26–28, 30–32, 55, 81, 137

Abrogation of the Mosaic Law, 57–59

Activism, political, 82, 139, 140

Adam, 16, 22–24, 30, 73, 131

Administration, 3, 6, 7, 10–11, 20, 39, 41, 45, 46, 55, 59, 69, 73, 76
  change of, 3, 7, 11, 12, 80

Adoption, 50, 93, 98, 104, 106

Adultery, 62

Advent
  First, 4–5, 11, 17, 19, 33, 36, 39, 41, 43, 44, 46, 50, 52–53, 59–60, 64
  Second, 10, 17, 18, 34, 44, 45, 53, 55, 67, 72, 74–75, 82, 134

Agrippa, 35

*Aion*, 10

Ambassador, 124, 126, 142

Angel, 6, 58, 66, 74, 87–88, 138
  fallen, 6, 7, 13, 42–43, 73, 75, 77, 78, 87
  of *Yahweh*, 5

Angelic conflict, 6, 7, 13, 42, 73, 90, 108, 122

Animal sacrifice, 24–25, 33, 57, 59, 116, 124

Anti-Semitism, 32, 34, 74

Antonine Caesars, 68

Archelaus, 35

Armageddon, 74

Ascension, 9 10, 39, 44, 64

Assets
  computer, 98, 104, 105, 108, 109, 111
  divine, 15, 63, 97, 102, 103, 106, 120, 122, 135
  personnel, 98, 119, 121, 122
  portfolio of invisible, 85, 97, 98, 104, 122, 128, 130, 133
  primary, 98, 104, 109, 110, 116, 117, 121
  production, 98, 111, 117–19
  secondary, 98, 109–12, 115, 117, 119, 121, 122
  for undeserved suffering, 98, 111, 119
  utilize, 20, 66, 86, 95, 102, 108, 112, 117, 120, 122, 141, 142
  volitional, 98, 111, 121

Athenians, 26, 54, 84

Authority
  divinely delegated, 11, 62
  of God. *See* God
  of husband, 23
  parental, 11, 25
  spiritual, 24


Babel, tower of, 25–26
Baptism of Fire, 75
Bible doctrine
  application of, 3, 43, 47, 58, 61,
    63, 70, 76, 79, 81, 89, 90, 95,
    96, 97, 100, 114–15, 119, 133,
    142
  basic, 115, 116, 141
  communication of, 55, 67, 70
  departing from, 115
  distracts from, 69
  dynamics of, 135, 139
  emphasis on, 70
  first priority of, 101, 117, 131
  ignorance of, 102
  impact of, 76
  importance of, 2, 3
  knowledge of, 1, 30, 95, 101, 112,
    115, 140
  learning, 1, 76, 89, 92, 100, 102,
    103, 110, 122, 123, 124, 125,
    135, 142
  love for, 112
  meditating upon, 97, 114
  neglect of, 102
  positive volition toward, 112
  reception, retention, and recall
    of, 2
  rejection of, 102
  respond to, 123
  solving problems with, 114

  teaching, 2, 34
  understood, 48, 112
Blessing
  by association, 137–39
  basis for, 127
  capacity for, 3, 102
  for the Church, 106–08
  distribution of, 99, 137, 138
  divine, 2, 25, 58, 67, 68, 72, 92,
    100, 111, 137, 140
  escrow, 98–104, 109, 111, 128,
    130, 138
  eternal, 32, 33
  in eternity, 100–03
  exceptional, 100
  government, 68
  guarantee of, 128, 130
  invisible, 111
  for Israel, 27, 35, 128
  logistical, 100
  loss of, 96
  national, 137, 138
  sign of, 128
  source of, 98
  spiritual, 97, 98, 100
  suffering for, 119, 121
  in time, 1, 100, 101, 102
  undistributed, 102, 103
Blood of Christ, 40, 62, 87
Body of Christ, 66, 86, 122, 135
Bright Morning Star, 66
Brutus, 83
Burning bush, 5


Cain, 25
Calvin, John, 140
Capital punishment, 62
Cassius, 83

Christian
  first-century, 84, 91
  influence, 47, 66, 136, 137
  responsibility, 20, 59, 60, 61, 63,
    68, 82, 115, 119, 136, 142
  service, 68, 92, 117-19, 125, 140,
    142
  way of life, 1–2, 3, 5, 11–13,
    19–21, 30, 46, 47, 48, 52, 56,
    58–61, 63, 66, 70, 76, 79, 85,
    88, 90, 93, 94, 96–98, 101–03,
    108, 109, 111, 115, 118, 128,
    140, 141
*Chronos*, 7, 10
Church
  Christ, 4–6, 9
  Head of the, 52, 108
  and Israel, 4, 11, 28, 39, 40, 43,
    45, 49, 53–56, 61, 80, 81, 93
  local, 69, 70, 119, 121, 125, 136
  Rapture of, 17–18, 54, 64, 71, 72,
    90, 101, 103, 135
  separation of state and, 59–61, 63,
    68, 136
  uniqueness of, 11–15, 20, 28, 31,
    43–45, 47, 48, 51, 54, 56, 58,
    60, 61, 64, 65, 68–70, 75–77, 93,
    94, 98, 99, 103–08, 113, 121–23,
    125–31, 133–38
  universal, 8, 12, 66, 67, 86
Church Age, 5, 7–15, 17, 19, 23, 26,
    30, 35, 41, 43–48, 50–54, 56–71,
    76, 77, 79, 81–83, 85–88, 90–99,
    102–09, 113, 114, 116, 117, 119,
    121–31, 133–39, 141, 142
Circumcision, 27
Client nation, 28, 34–36, 57, 61, 62,
    64, 66–69, 74–76, 136, 138

Code
  establishment, 29, 31–34, 40, 57,
    62–63
  freedom, 32, 33, 34, 40, 57, 61
  of Hamurabi, 33
  new, 30, 58
  spiritual, 29, 31–34, 40, 57, 62
Confession, 88, 132
Constitution of the United States, 61
Continuity, 12, 15, 23, 25, 27, 30,
    77, 79–81, 107, 119, 128, 139
Cornerstone, 49, 53–56
Covenant, 8, 25, 26
  Abrahamic, 26, 27, 31, 34
  conditional, 32, 40
  Davidic, 31, 32, 34, 39, 52
  everlasting, 32
  New, 31, 32, 34
  Palestinian, 28, 31, 34
  promises, 81
  unconditional, 8, 27, 32–34, 40,
    44, 67, 73, 74, 80
Crassus, 35
Crowns, 102
Cult of
  Dionysus, 96
  Isis, 12

Daniel, 72, 137
  seventieth week of, 72
David, 5, 8, 30, 40, 45, 53, 65, 66,
    131, 137, 139
Death
  spiritual, 87
  substitutionary, 10, 34, 39–42, 51,
    62, 113, 141
Degeneracy, spiritual, 35, 36, 59
Destiny
  personal sense of, 52, 100, 122

royal, 142
special, 98, 107
spiritual, 2, 57, 103, 106, 115
Dichotomous, 24
Discipline, 17, 27, 32, 35, 44, 67,
    69, 72, 73, 90, 103, 109, 121,
    134, 137
Dispensations
  between, 6, 10, 13, 15, 45, 58, 60,
    77
  christocentric, 4, 17, 37–70, 107
  definition of, 3, 4, 6, 10–15, 19
  divisions of, 4, 7, 9, 11, 16
  eschatological, 5, 18, 71–78
  theocentric, 4, 16, 23–35
Divine decree, 41, 42, 94, 104, 105,
    110–11
Divine dynasphere, 51, 52, 56, 58,
    66, 86, 88–90, 94, 100, 108, 110,
    112, 114, 117–18, 123–25, 128,
    131–33, 141
  operational, 52, 56, 58, 66, 88, 94,
    123, 133, 141
  prototype, 52, 56, 58, 66, 88, 141
Divine institutions, 23, 28
  family, 28
  marriage, 23
  national entity, 28
  volition, 23
Divine viewpoint, 1, 3, 16, 49, 80,
    95, 140

Ecstatics, 76–77, 91
Elect people, 31, 32
Election
  of Christ, 92, 107
  of Church, 68, 98, 104–08, 122,
    123
  of Israel, 68, 107

  for salvation, 106
Elijah, 74
Emotionalism, 139, 140
Encouragement, 25, 27, 47, 68, 90,
    116, 136
Equal
  opportunity, 102, 122, 123, 137
  privilege, 88, 102, 122, 123, 137
Equality, 85, 122–23
Establishment, laws of divine, 27,
    30–33, 40, 57, 61–63, 67, 72, 119
Eternal state, 18, 43, 75, 78, 123
Ethics, 32, 48, 57, 58
Evangelism, 55, 67, 69
Eve, 24, 30
Evidence testing, 120, 138
Evil, 7, 23, 25–26, 46, 47, 72, 95,
    115, 131, 139

Faith
  of Abraham, 28, 55
  in Christ, 1, 5, 6, 24, 25, 28, 33,
    62, 78, 87, 92, 93, 96, 106, 112,
    113, 140
Faith-rest, 47, 52
Fall of man, 16, 23–25, 76
Filling of the Holy Spirit, 52, 76,
    132
Flood, the, 25, 26
Foundation, invisible, 54, 55, 112,
    115
Frame of reference, 3, 59, 79, 112,
    115, 137
Free will, 42, 62, 104, 105, 109,
    110, 123, 136
Freedom, 26, 29, 34, 62, 63, 67
  of choice, 41, 110
  human, 33, 40, 61
  spiritual, 63, 106, 130, 142

Garden of Eden, 22–24, 73

Gentile nations, 66–68, 136

Gentiles, 14, 16, 25, 31, 36, 45, 46, 58, 75, 86, 91, 124
  dispensations of the, 4, 11, 22, 30, 37, 134
  times of the, 7, 67

God
  authority of, 7, 12, 23, 40
  character of, 6, 19, 58, 62, 81
  confidence in, 27, 115, 116, 121
  faithfulness of, 27, 30, 32, 57, 62, 80, 81, 90, 102
  fellowship with, 30, 78, 88, 89, 132
  glory of, 2, 19, 102, 128–38
  happiness of, 51, 52, 141
  love of, 40, 42, 55, 90, 104, 127
  nature of, 2, 38, 41, 88
  plan of, 10, 15, 20, 26, 30, 43, 51, 56, 58–59, 66, 80, 82, 85, 88, 90, 93–97, 101, 102, 107-10, 116–17, 120, 121–23, 129, 130, 133, 137, 139, 141, 142
  presence of, 29, 128, 130
  promises of, 5, 8, 24–27, 29, 30, 32, 34, 40, 46, 49, 56, 59, 72, 73, 80, 81, 102, 135
  purpose of, 2, 3, 9, 19, 26, 46, 79, 80, 85, 87, 99, 104, 107–08, 110, 116, 121, 127, 129, 135
  relationship with, 5, 9, 24–25, 63, 82, 86, 92–94, 95, 100, 113, 115, 131
  universal knowledge of, 76

Godliness, 90

Gog and Magog, 77

Good
  deeds, 140
  of intrinsic value, 117–19

Gospel, 5, 25, 34, 36, 42, 50, 68, 73, 74, 113, 125

Gospels, 39–44, 48

Government, 26, 33, 63, 67, 68, 77, 119

Grace, 4, 5, 7, 13, 14, 19, 20, 24, 25, 29, 30, 33, 36, 42–43, 45, 50, 52, 57, 59, 60, 64, 70, 74, 77, 78, 81, 82, 91, 92, 95–97, 103, 104, 109, 110, 112–16, 118–20, 128, 133, 138
  dying, 111
  greater, 3, 100
  logistical, 47, 100, 102, 117, 123, 126
  orientation, 52, 96

Ham, 25

Heavenly citizenship, 85, 97

Heritage
  eternal, 27
  impact, 139
  of Israel, 8, 27, 28, 30, 45
  of a nation, 63
  spiritual, 96

Hermeneutics, 48

Herod, 35

Historical trends, 136

History
  biblical, 6, 23, 63
  control of, 60, 133, 135, 136
  divine view of, 3, 16, 80
  human, 3–7, 10, 11, 24, 27, 30, 37, 39, 42, 43, 48, 52, 55, 58, 62, 64–66, 70, 77, 80, 82, 96, 105, 108, 133, 136, 137, 142
  interpretation of, 3, 4, 134
  period of, 20, 39, 48, 50, 72

Holy days, 24, 57, 59
Holy of Holies, 35
Holy Spirit
  baptism of, 14, 56, 85–87, 91–93,
    97, 117, 122, 123
  deity of, 130
  enduement of, 133
  filling of, 48, 76, 88–91, 111,
    130–33
  fruit of, 88, 89
  grieving of, 89, 132
  indwelling. See Indwelling of
  ministry of, 9, 48, 51, 76, 86, 88,
    121, 129, 133
  power of, 58, 63, 95, 113, 114,
    128, 130, 141
  quenching of, 89, 132
  renewing by, 131
  teaching of, 114
  walking in, 48, 88, 114
Homosexuality, 63
Hoshea, 17
Human merit, 92, 95, 121
Human spirit, 24
Hypostatic union, 37–39, 65, 86, 95
  dispensation of, 5, 9, 17, 19, 35,
    37, 39, 40, 47–53, 55, 56, 59,
    66, 71, 77, 86, 128–29, 134

Illumination, 114, 130, 133
Immanence, 127
Imputation, 92
Incarnation, 4, 5, 9, 13, 17, 19,
    48–49, 51–54, 59, 64, 129
Indwelling of
  believer's body, 127
  Christ, 15, 45, 127–31
  God the Father, 126–28
  God the Holy Spirit, 127, 131–32

  the Trinity, 85, 126
Internationalism, 26
Invisible heroes, 85, 134, 137, 138,
    142
  foundation of, 112
  impact of, 60, 66, 67, 76, 82, 88,
    96, 130, 136–39, 142
  influence of, 47, 66, 72–73, 136,
    137
  palace of, 94, 123
  power of, 115
  resources of, 116, 120, 136, 138,
    142
  the work of God, 112
Isaac, 27, 28, 30, 32
Isaiah, 69, 75, 91, 129
Israel, 4, 7–9, 11, 13, 14, 17, 27–36,
    39–41, 43–47, 52–56, 58, 60–69,
    73–76, 80–82, 91, 93, 94, 107,
    128, 129, 134, 135
  national future of, 40, 44
  spiritual, 80, 81

Jacob, 27, 28, 30, 32, 72
Japheth, 25
Jeroboam, 17
Jewish Age, 7, 9, 19, 28
Jewish evangelists, 74, 107
Judah
  nation of, 17
  tribe of, 30
Judea, 8, 35–36, 44
Judgment
  divine, 6, 50, 76, 141
  eternal, 78, 116
  Last, 75, 78
  national, 91
  seat of Christ, 101, 118
Julius Caesar, 83

Juvenile delinquency, 61–62

*Kairos*, 7, 10
King of kings, 66, 75, 87
Kingdom
  of God, 8, 10, 13, 39–41, 43, 46,
    59, 65, 82, 138
  millennial, 59
  Northern, 17
  Southern, 17
  Theocratic, 17, 29
  United, 17
  utopian, 74
*Kleroi*, 84

Lake of fire, 78
Land, 26, 29, 31, 32, 34
Law
  of Christ, 58, 61–62
  civil, 61
  divine, 58, 61
  fulfilled, 30, 33, 40, 51, 52, 56, 58,
    59, 62, 63
  of Moses, 20, 21, 29–34, 40, 46,
    47, 51, 56–63, 124
  volitional responsibility, 121
Legalism, 35, 46, 59, 81, 90, 118,
  141
Love
  personal for God, 52, 100, 102,
    112, 118
  system of, 90
Luther, Martin, 140

Macedonia, 83
Magna Carta, 61
Mark Antony, 83
Messiah, 5, 13, 25, 27, 29, 30, 32,
  33, 35–36, 40, 41, 43–47, 49, 52,
  61–62

Microchip, 104–05
  PROM, 105–06, 109, 123
  ROM, 105, 109, 123
Military, 33, 35, 119
Millennium, 5, 8, 11, 13, 18, 34, 44,
  46, 47, 52, 55, 59, 60, 71–77,
  82, 134
Mind of Christ, 2, 88, 89, 130, 131
Missionary
  agency, 25, 28, 67, 74
  service, 119
Momentum testing, 102, 120
Morality, 56, 140
Mosaic law. *See* law of Moses
Moses, 16, 23, 24, 28, 29, 59, 61,
  63, 74, 137
Mystery cults, 12
Mystery doctrine, 12–15, 20, 43, 60,
  69, 70, 81, 85, 87, 94, 96–97,
  114, 122, 126, 142

Names of Christ, 5
Nehemiah, 17
New spiritual species, 15, 60, 85–86,
  106–07, 117, 129
Noah, 25, 30

Obedience, 20, 23, 27, 57, 61, 90,
  110
Occupation with Christ, 52, 131
Octavian, 83
Offerings, 29
*Oikonomia*, 11
Olivet Discourse, 18, 40, 44, 72

Passover lamb, 29
Pastor, 2, 69, 122, 125
Patriarchs, 16

Age of the Jewish, 16, 22, 26–28, 31
Paul, the Apostle, 9–10, 12–14, 26, 54, 67, 69, 83, 84, 93, 96, 135
Peace, universal, 76
Pentecost, 64
Peter, the Apostle, 9
Pharisees, 35, 46, 47
Philippi, 83–84
Pillar of fire, 5, 128
Pivot, 47, 67, 68, 73, 133, 138
Plato, 11
*Politeuma*, 82–85, 97, 98–107
  metaphor, 81–84, 88
Pompey, 35
Pontius Pilate, 36
Positional sanctification, 87–88, 92
  current, 87
  retroactive, 87
Postcanon period, 18, 68–70, 77, 134–35
Power
  divine, 6, 13, 42, 43, 52, 58, 63, 64, 66, 70, 77, 82, 85, 88, 90, 95, 108, 113–15, 117, 118, 121, 128, 130, 133, 134, 141–42
  great experiment, 50–52, 65, 66, 86, 95–97, 137
  human, 6, 95, 113, 117, 118
  political, 72, 74
  seat of, 123
  source of, 51, 132
  system of, 13, 49, 51, 56, 65, 86, 88–90, 133
Prayer, 47, 68, 124
Precanon period, 18, 68–70, 134
Precedent, 5, 21, 52, 56, 58, 94
Predestination, 96, 98, 104–06, 108, 122–23

Priesthood
  of Christ, 92, 124
  family, 24, 25
  holy, 54
  Levitical, 29, 30, 33, 59, 124
  privacy of, 58, 125
  royal, 124, 125
  universal, 59, 123–25
Privacy, 26, 34, 58, 62, 67, 124–25
Privileges, 15, 35, 60, 64–65, 67, 83–85, 93, 97, 107–08, 124
Problem-solving devices, 51–52, 66, 70, 112, 120, 141
Progressive revelation, 81
Property, 26, 62, 67
Prophecy, 10, 12, 13, 39, 40, 69, 72, 75, 85, 86, 133–36
  absence of, 85, 134–36
Protocol plan of God, 30, 43, 56, 58, 60, 63, 85, 88–90, 93–98, 101, 102, 106, 108–10, 112, 116–18, 121–24, 127–31, 133, 137, 139, 141, 142
Providential preventive suffering, 120

Racial discrimination, 88
Rapture, 17–18, 53, 54, 64, 71, 72, 90, 101, 126, 134, 135
Rebound, 52, 103, 120, 132
Regenerate, 24, 27, 28, 32, 46, 73, 80, 81, 131
Rehoboam, 17
Remnant of Israel, 11, 43, 74
Resurrection, 13, 17, 39, 42, 49, 53, 60, 64, 71, 75, 77, 90, 103, 113, 134, 135, 141
  body, 39, 53–55, 75, 77, 90, 103
Resuscitation, 53, 74

Ritual, 21, 24, 27, 29–30, 33, 52, 57, 62, 70, 76, 94, 116, 124, 129
Roman
 adoption, 93, 98, 104
 aristocracy, 93
 armies, 35–36, 83
 citizen, 83–84
 colony, 83
 Empire, 8, 35–36, 41, 61, 67–69
 Republic, 83–85
 soldiers, 84
Royal commissions, 85, 124–26
Royal family, 53, 62, 64–66, 68, 70–72, 75, 79, 81, 85, 86, 92–94, 96, 97, 106, 107, 112, 121–23, 126, 129, 133, 136–37, 139, 142
Royalty
 battlefield, 66, 107, 108
 divine, 65, 92
 Jewish, 65
 spiritual, 66, 86, 92–94, 105, 108, 124

Sabbath, 44, 59, 60, 62
Salvation
 after, 1–3, 15, 65, 79, 88, 90–92, 95, 101, 107, 112–14, 139, 140, 142
 agent of, 106, 113
 appropriation of, 5
 cause of, 106, 113
 eternal, 1, 6, 106, 113
 by grace, 77
 loss of, 96, 102, 110
 means of, 25, 28
 moment of, 85, 88, 91–93, 107, 111–12, 121–23, 125, 126, 132
 provide, 40, 129
 purchase of, 41, 49, 50–52, 107

 way of, 15, 33, 42, 46, 55
Sanctification, 86–87, 92, 106
 experiential, 88–90, 104
 positional, 87, 88, 92
 ultimate, 90, 104
Sanhedrin, 35
Satan, 6, 7, 13, 18, 23, 42, 43, 46, 53, 66, 72–75, 77, 82, 87, 89, 95–96, 120, 138, 139
 cosmic system of, 89, 95–96
 trial of, 6–7, 42–43, 73, 77, 120, 138
Saul, 17
Second Triumvirate, 83
Seed
 of Abraham, 27, 81
 of the woman, 24, 30
Sermon on the Mount, 45–48, 59, 75, 79
Sharing with Christ, 3, 87, 92
Shekinah Glory, 128–31
Shem, 25
Sin, 23, 24, 34, 40, 41, 50–52, 61–62, 66, 77, 88, 95, 125, 129, 132
Sin nature, 95, 115, 119, 131, 132
Sovereignty, 42, 105, 106–07, 109, 123
 expressions of, 107
 provisions of, 123
Spiritual adulthood, 55, 116, 118–21, 124
Spiritual autonomy, 115–16, 120
Spiritual childhood, 117
Spiritual gifts, 69, 91, 98, 121–22, 125
 administration, 122
 permanent, 69
 temporary, 69

Spiritual growth, 2, 4, 9, 20, 70, 89, 92, 101–02, 112, 113, 116–20, 122, 124–25, 135
Spiritual maturity, 2, 27, 56, 70, 82, 100–02, 111, 112, 116, 120, 129, 130, 133, 137
Spiritual self-esteem, 52, 116, 120–21

Tabernacle, 29, 33, 54, 128–29
Ten Commandments, 31, 60–61, 79
Theocracy, 56, 68, 135–36
Theophanies, 24
Thinking, 1, 89, 90, 113, 115, 140
    of Christ, 2–3, 114
    establishment, 57, 63
Tithing, 59
Tongues, 36, 69, 91
Transcendence, 127
Transfiguration, 128–29
Tree of the knowledge of good and evil, 23
Tribulation, 5, 7, 11, 17, 18, 40, 44, 53, 55, 71–76, 107, 126, 134, 135
Trichotomous, 24

Types, 30

Union with Christ, 6, 63, 85–88, 92–93, 97, 104, 106, 111, 117, 123, 124, 135
Upper Room Discourse, 12, 18, 43–44, 48, 60, 136

Virgin birth, 16, 35, 37, 39, 65
Volition, 23, 25, 28, 41, 51, 90, 101, 103–06, 109–11, 121–23, 132
    Age of Negative, 16
    Age of Positive, 16
    negative, 24–25, 42, 103, 109, 115, 116, 126
    positive, 22, 23, 47, 109, 111–16, 118, 119, 136

Witnessing, 119

Xenophon, 11

Zedekiah, 17
Zwingli, 140

NOTES

NOTES